The TOP SECRET
Tory Handbook

what every new MP must know *

D1637482

LESTER
&ORPEN
DENNYS
PUBLISHERS

*and what every Canadian *should* know

Copyright © 1984 by Osher, Inc.
All rights reserved.

Canadian Cataloguing in Publication Data

Main entry under title:
The Top-secret Tory handbook

ISBN 0-88619-066-5

1. Progressive Conservative Party of Canada –
Anecdotes, facetiae, satire, etc.

PN6231.P6T66 1984   324.27104'02'07   C84-099132-0

Design: Public Good
Printed and bound in Canada by:
Imprimerie Gagné Ltée.

Lester & Orpen Dennys Limited
78 Sullivan Street
Toronto, Ontario M5T 1C1

Table of Contents

Introduction

As the hundreds of new Tory members of Parliament know, this book has been privately circulated in manuscript form for over a year, on the assumption that we would achieve a majority government.

Now that we have — in spades — I approached the publisher, who rushed it into print. He felt, as I do, that, as a matter of public record, this manuscript should be made available to all Canadians, including even the handful who didn't vote Tory on September 4.

The *Tory Handbook* describes the Tory style — that Great Blue Rinse which will wash the country clean — which we trust will rule in Ottawa well into the nineties.

Although this handbook is primarily for new MPs, it's really for everyone who wishes to eat, drink, sleep, even think Tory for the rest of the century.

The media have labelled 1984 "Orwell's Year". But we know that it is really *Brian's* year. And he'll be watching you, too.

"Deep Chin"
September, 1984

CHAPTER ONE

Our Leader

How to Pronounce Our New Leader's Name

First Name: It should be noted that Brian is *not* spelled with a y, as in Bryan. This would be too snooty, too exclusive, too conservative. No, his name is spelled B-r-i-a-n, like the Common Man background he prides himself on having. He is the Boy from Baie Comeau, and don't you forget it. As we put it, "It's hard not to think of the Baie."

The Pronunciation of Our Leader's First Name: This is important. Occasionally you'll run into a Brian who uses some coy, obnoxious, elitist, ethnic pronunciation, such as the Canadian novelist Brian Moore, whom you probably haven't heard of; he was born in Ireland and lives in the States, but he wrote a few books with Canadian landscapes in them so we claim him as one of us. Anyway, Moore pronounces his name Bree-an as in Flea-ban.

Not our Leader. Not on your life. He pronounces it Briii-anne, as in Cry-ran, which is what the Grits (rest in peace) and the Socialists did after the election! He's just a regular sort of guy, who has happened to be blessed with wealth, good looks, a stunning wife, and bright, healthy children. You should be so lucky. Just call him Brian. Plain, ordinary Brian. That is, if you are in the Cabinet. If you are a back-bencher, call him Mr. Mulroney. Which leads to the next concern:

The Pronunciation of Our Leader's Last Name: It seems that nearly everyone gets it wrong, when it's really quite easy and simple. It's three syllables, just as ancient Gaul was divided, if you remember your high school Latin.

Anyway, it's *not* pronounced Mull-rone-ee, as in Baloney, which is the way most newscasters still do it.

And it's *not* pronounced Mule-runny, as in Cool-bunny, which is the way a number of other newscasters pronounce it.

No, it's merely pronounced Mull-roo-nee, as in Cartoony.

Do you have it straight now? Briii-anne Mull-roo-nee. It's really not so hard, is it?

And if he's going to be our Leader for the next dozen years or so, at the very least, then the very least *you* can do is to learn how to get it *right*.

You want incentive to pronounce it? (And you *know* how important incentive is to Tory thought; it's the NDP that destroys incentive, through their criminal socialistic policies.)

Just try pronouncing this a few times: Sen-et. As in Bennett. Sen-et. Sen-et. Sen-et. We even recommend it as a mantra, to be used in lieu of the one the Maharishi gave you, to practise TM in the a.m. and the p.m.

You want to end up in the Sen-et? Then say Briii-anne Mull-roo-nee, and say it right, and say it often, and don't use it in vain, and who knows. *You* could win Cash for Life!!!!

A Few Words on My Dear Brian

by the "First Lady"

I was asked to write a few words to welcome all of you new Members of Parliament to Ottawa. It wasn't easy for me to find the time, what with all the redecorating of 24 Sussex, shampooing, combing, brushing, brushing, brushing, and caring for my three darling children and all, but I finally managed to sit down and do it.

What can I say? That each and every one of you will learn to love Brian just as much as I do? That he will probably become to each of you what he has been to me and our children – a loving father, a true friend, an idol, a god?

Perhaps I should go back a bit, to that first time I saw Brian at that swimming pool. There I was, just a child, and there he was, towering, handsome, a successful lawyer, the sun reflecting gloriously off his chin. And when he dived into the water, and talked to me by the diving board, his chin appeared even larger and longer than it had before, due to the effect of the water's magnification. (I know all this from my years in engineering, which I so willingly gave up in order to be with Brian and bear his children. Our children. His children.)

Of course, I hope to go back to school and finish my degree in engineering, but I plan to wait until the children are older, like maybe in their thirties. I'll still be less than sixty then, with many years of fruitful and creative work ahead of me. But since Brian will probably still be Prime Minister of this magnificent land, maybe I'll put it off again, and continue to support him as his helpmate.

As I know that all of *you* will do, as well. I've never forgotten how you voted to make his victory unanimous, back in June of 1983. It warmed the cockles of my heart, if you'll pardon the expression, to see so many men, and a growing number of women as well, which is a nice sign, support the man who has carried us to glory, and who will continue to run our country so well, well into the next century.

I have been proud and happy to give my all and everything to him, and I am sure that you feel the same way. Together, we can make this country great again, and work together to make the twenty-first century belong to Canada.

Brian is a giving, loving, kindly man. I only pray that you will get to know him as warmly and as intimately as I have. Well, maybe not that much, but you know what I mean.

And know that he will give, if you are willing to give. Unlike that wretched man who almost ruined our Great Country back in the 1970s, and right into this decade, Brian is a magnificent compromiser; a man of give and take. Look at myself, for instance. All I did was give up my career, my life's work, my self-image, and Brian has just as easily and willingly given up drinking and smoking. Well, he *promised*!

Stand by him. Learn to love him as I have (and do!) Let us have no more blood-letting! Look what happened to Dief and Joe! No more! Not by the hair of his chinny-chin-chin!

Together, we can make this world a better place to live in for all men of good will.*

M.

Who's Who in Brian's Cabinet**

As noted above, Canada is a country whose government is truly run by Cabinet, in spite of what commies, leftists, and bleeding-heart liberals may say about democracy, republics, and so on. Getting into the Cabinet may seem as difficult as a camel getting through the eye of a needle (if you don't recognize that line, you've been using your hotel rooms for the wrong reasons), but it really isn't. As you can see from the list below, there are literally dozens and dozens of Cabinet jobs, if you've been on the right side of Brian (figuratively).

Should you have the blessed good fortune of receiving this first step towards the Senate, you have an obligation to know what your duties will be. Here they are:

External Affairs: If you assumed this means having girls in every port, you are not cut out for the job. If you think Namibia is a soothing ointment, you are also not fit. Basically, the Minister for External Affairs must know *exactly* where the United States tells us to stand in world politics.

---

* Yes, yes, some women too, who never married, or who *have* to work. But there are really so few, I didn't think it necessary to mention them. Brian asked me to, so I did.

**Job descriptions obtained from Grits-Canada.

Solicitor-General: Someone easily confused by the written word. Your job would be to supply wienies and marshmallows for RCMP barn-burnings.

Public Works: Don't panic; your job would *not* entail making sure that the public works. In fact, you would be basically in charge of Crystal Palaces in Ottawa and landing-strips for 747s in the ridings of each of the other Cabinet Ministers.

Employment and Immigration: This may seem like a contradiction in terms at first; after all, if we let immigrants in, they will take jobs away from real Canadians, right?

Right. Then again, immigrants tend to take only the jobs which Canadians refuse to take, since they are considered beneath them: dishwasher, cook, waiter/waitress, nurse, doctor, lawyer, scientist, poet, novelist, teacher, etc. Still, relatively high immigration need not be a threat to Canada, since if the newcomers were that good, they would have gone to the States. Furthermore, they and their descendants tend to be so ecstatic about being let into our country that they will vote for the party which let them in. It worked for the Grits, didn't it?

Treasury Board: Represented by an individual who is incapable of bringing himself to shriek, "Stop the presses!"

Finance: For this position, you would need all the answers to our problems and none of the solutions. At least once a year, sometimes twice, you would have to attempt to pull the polyester over the eyes of the public, wool being far too expensive nowadays.

National Defence: A contradiction of terms, but a necessary one. (See Chapter Six.)

Industry, Trade and Commerce: To hold this position adequately, you would have to know and use the latest techno-jargon for "hewers of wood, drawers of water".

Regional Economic Expansion: That depends upon the region, and how they voted in the last election. Due to severe cutbacks, this department has become one of the tiniest in the government. As of late 1984, it consists of a Deputy Minister, rented from Finance, who advises his Minister as to where the next UIC office shall be opened. (And where it will be reopened after the next cutback.)

Energy, Mines and Resources: Keep Dome alive, Petro-Can in the black, and the public in the dark. What is mined is ours, and what is ours is mined.

National Revenue: Originally Archeology Canada, this department is expected to discover more skeletons than the Leakey family. Motto: "Big Bother is Watching You." The Minister should resemble J. Edgar Hoover and answer to the nickname "Stonewall". The Grits really loused up this department, by going after writers, artists, dentists, and small businessmen. We would expect our Minister to go after socialist writers and artists, and Liberal dentists and small businessmen. (The big businessmen are on our side, and *don't you forget it*.) Skeptical is the overriding attitude.

Justice: Not in our lifetime. In charge of Spy Canada. If you avoid paying off murderers for squealing, and letting convicted rapists get day-passes to feminist conventions, you'll do fine.

Indian Affairs and Northern Development: As the Treasury Board and the Finance Minister will be pleased to inform you, our treaties with the First Nations are worth approximately the paper they are printed on. As far as the second half of this portfolio is concerned, since over 90% of Canadians live within a hundred miles of the American border, your duties include the development of Kelowna, Edmonton, Gimli, and Muskoka cottage country (north of Toronto). If Quebec doesn't stay heavily Tory in the next few elections and by-elections, it doesn't get a penny. (See also Chapter Seven.)

Labour: Since, from 1968, the Grits eliminated most of this, we might drop it.

Clerk of the Privy Council: Johnny on the Spot. Next to the Queen and Brian, this is where the action is.

Health and Welfare: Health is fine, but the welfare will have to stop.

Secretary of State: We haven't the slightest idea, except that you get to travel a lot for free.

Fisheries and Oceans: In a sentence, the offshore fields belong to Ottawa, not to the provinces. A complex portfolio, ever since Brigitte Bardot gave her seal of approval to approving seals. More on this later.

Agriculture: If the price is right, sell wheat to Gaddafi. If the price is right, sell wheat to South Africa. If the price is right, sell wheat to Albania. If the price is low enough, pay the farmers not to sell wheat to Canadians; they eat too much anyway.

Veterans' Affairs: Since there are only a few dozen left, this might be absorbed into National Revenue. That should wipe them out better than the Axis ever managed to do.

Consumer and Corporate Affairs: Making sure pop bottles don't explode and fire-crackers do. Be more concerned about the latter; there are a fair number of consumers in this country, but it's the corporations who give us the money to keep going. We are Tories, and don't you forget it.

Transport: Making sure every Cabinet Minister and his spouse (and girlfriend, if you keep your fat trap shut) get free passes on Air Canada. See Public Works.

Economic Development: Fat chance. But if you really want to take a stab at it, see Treasury Board, above.

Environment: Be for it, unless it comes into contact with Public Works; Employment and Immigration; Industry, Trade and Commerce; Regional Economic Expansion; Energy, Mines and Resources; Indian Affairs and Northern Development; Labour; Fisheries and Oceans; Agriculture; Consumer and Corporate Affairs; Transport; or Economic Development. Remember the snail-darter in the States; if you get little Ralph Naders running around, our economy will start to look like October 1929, Part II.

Science and Technology: Be for both. Talk silicon chips, RAMs, ROMs, lasers, and the other big words. Don't make mention of how

The Wrong Stuff

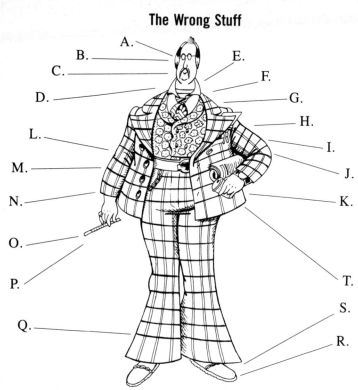

A. Presley-vestige hairstyle. B. Glasses *circa* 1957 . . . usually with tape binding one earpiece to front frame. C. Fu Manchu. D. T-shirt with beer logo showing through dress shirt. E. 15½ neck on an 18½ neck. F. 1964 tie patterned on flag of British Columbia on acid. G. Brocade, gambler-style vest. H. More buttons than in a high-rise elevator. I. Pocket-hankie, cardboard dry-cleaning advert. J. Collection of ballpoint pens — two of which, when turned upside down, show woman losing clothes. K. Coffee, double double, in Styrofoam cup, leaking, sipped through hole punched in plastic lid. L. White vinyl belt, gathered by large belt-buckle depicting a Nevada sunset rendered in iridescent mica slices. M. Buckle pushed to one hip. N. Biker chain, attached to wallet carried in back pocket. O. Old Port cigar with candied tip. P. Large pinky ring. Q. Bell-bottoms. Suit pattern: game board. R. White loafers with gold chains. S. Crêpe soles. T. Newspaper in jacket pocket: *National Enquirer.*

BRIAN STYLE: The Right Stuff

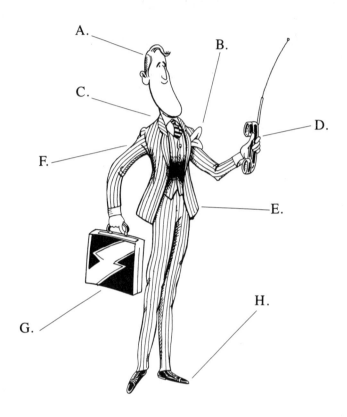

A. High profile; hair and make-up by Mila
B. Silk pocket handkerchief depicting Celtic charm and Slavic high style
C. Le Chef silk foulard necktie, with Pivnicki knot
D. F.C.C. (Fat City Connections) mobile telephone
E. The Presidential Chivas Regal Blue — A classic 5 piece.
    (a) Vest   (b) Jacket   (c) Trousers
    (d) Undervest   (e) Knickers, unknotted
F. Turnbull & Asser Oxford cotton shirt, barrel cuffs by Le Porc
G. Gucci briefcase. Contents: 2 cartons Du Maurier Grand Luxe Cigarettes, Irish songs and blarney policies
H. Black classic lace-ups, from East of Centre Block Shoes

Mitel, Nabu, Develcon, and all the other Canadian hi-tech firms have had their stocks crash through the floor. Just quote endlessly from McLuhan or, better yet, since he's not Canadian, Alvin Toffler, and you'll thrive.

Social Development: Far too early. Girls shouldn't be dating until they are into their teens; boys shouldn't get the family car until eighteen. What's happened to our morality, anyway?

Communications: See Science and Technology. For a lot of inexplicable reasons, they have become one and the same over the past few years.

Supply and Services: See the film *Hookers on Davie*; it appears that Vancouver has managed to combine the two quite well.

Minister Without Portfolio: This does not mean that you had your luggage stolen. It merely means that Brian owes you some personal or private debts, is not certain exactly what to do with you, and you're too young for the Senate. Don't worry your pretty head about it; just go to the meetings, smile a lot, accept the extra money with grace and report it to Revenue Canada without rancour. That's half the battle, already.

CHAPTER TWO

Ottawa — City of Your Dreams

Where to Live in Ottawa

We realize that the phrase "where to live in Ottawa" may seem like a contradiction in terms, especially if you come from a swinging part of the country such as northern Alberta, or Labrador.

But there is much to be said for knowing just where to own, or rent, or squat, a house in the capital city. This is, after all, a capitalist, consumerist society (no matter how hard the Grits struggled to change all that), and you will be judged on where you and your family dwell.

If you have money, a Cabinet position, or Parliamentary Secretary status, consider these areas:

Rockcliffe Park Village
Alta Vista
New Edinburgh (Old Edinburgh being too far to commute)
Lower Town (Even though you'd probably be happier if it were called Upper Town. As a great man once said, "You can't always get what you want.")

Other suitable places to live:

The Canal Area, a.k.a. The Driveway
Centre Town

The Glebe (No relation to *The Mail*)
Ottawa South

Still others:

Sandy Hill
Ottawa East
Ottawa West
The bar in the Château Laurier (Cock & Lion)

Let it be noted that bunking in with other novice back-benchers, even those affiliated with the opposition party/ies, *is* tolerated. Yes, you're right; politics can make very strange bedfellows indeed. Just keep in your own bed.

You'd be surprised at the number of (very) odd couples sharing flats, apartments, and houses on the outskirts of respectability, which is a suburb of Ottawa.

Remember, you are *not* living in sin. You are living in Ottawa.

Sin is across the river.

What to Drive in Ottawa

If you are what you eat, according to the dietitians, then you are what you drive, according to the CAA. And you want to look intelligent, alert, economical, cool, *in*. Which is why all Tory MPs should drive:

1) A Volvo
2) A Toyota
3) A BMW (Cabinet Ministers — a must!)
4) Anything foreign that is in the guise of a station-wagon

Why no Canadian autos, you ask? First, with our Canadian labour record, it only seems fair that we demand something that works. But more important, we are Members of Parliament — a select group, elected by our lessers. We deserve the *best*.

(To be fair, a token Chrysler mini-van may be driven, as a nod to Lee Iacocca for a job well done and to cover our respective rears with the UAW, which doesn't usually vote PC anyway.)

What You Should Not Drive in Ottawa

1) Rickshaws (There *are* some about, but only for tourists)
2) Red River Wagons
3) Ladas. Remember Afghanistan! (You *do* remember Afghanistan, don't you?)
4) Note to Saskatchewan MPs: It is considered bad taste to park a harvester or combine in your driveway. Ditto any machinery by John Deere or Massey-Ferguson, please.
5) Note to Quebec MPs: Of course we know you would not drive a car with fuzzy dice hanging from the rear-view mirror, or a big furry dog in the back well, sitting in a homemade crèche of St. Christopher among the Wrecks, whose eyes light up when you slam down the brakes. But please, please, no 1956 Buicks!

Brian puts a lot of importance on how we present ourselves to the outside world, okay guys? You too, ladies.

What to Do with Stornoway

We have a dual response for this one. Take your pick:
1) Who cares?
2) To quote a former politician, or at least paraphrase him: "Where's Stornoway?"

The Best Embassies for a Good Time

Temperate economic times have severely curtailed the embassy gay social swirl, not to mention the straight one. Zena Cherry, in town recently, covered all the toniest embassy affairs in less than an hour, recording all the VIPs of note on the back of a single envelope. And that included their wives, too.

Ms. Cherry, not one to cause waves of criticism to lap at the foundations of high society, gave permission for her report to appear only in the regional editions of Canada's National Newspaper, thus sparing Toronto the stultifying boredom.

So what to do for a good time?

First, call Baron Benfinck, the First Secretary of the Dutch trade delegation.

Or Lord Moran (please don't slip and blurt "moron", although he is reputed to give cause), the British High Commissioner, who has definite party possibilities.

Or Paul Robinson at the American Embassy, where acid reigns supreme. Into his cups a little, he occasionally regresses to his former occupation, that of an insurance salesman, and attempts to interest you and your wife in a little protection. Considering whom he works for, it might not be a bad idea to give it some serious thought. Although, to be frank, the sight of anyone having a serious thought around Robinson or the American Embassy could be rather threatening. This is, after all, the government that gave the world James Watt and Ed Meese, is it not?

Forget the Chinese Embassy, no matter what your predilections are for their *basse cuisine*. You expected good food? At this place, even the mushrooms are canned. Hold the MSG, and hold the visits to a minimum.

The Russian Embassy is fine if you can bear all that red all over the place. (If you think Prince Igor has no taste, wait till you get inside *this* dump.) And when you find a bug in the salad they serve you *here*, it's the kind that listens, and is never, ever dead.

And do you really want to hang around a place where they feature a songstress who leads the revellers in hometown sing-songs such as "I Weep when I Remember Minsk" or "Don't Cry for Me, Vladivostok"?

(A word to the wise: these days, the Soviets are anxious to obtain and possess the most advanced electronic hardware and software, and the latest futurist data on same. So if an invitation is sent to you requesting your presence for cocktails and "fragments" (not shrapnel, but Rus-

sianese for hors d'oeuvres), be careful what you say about Kanata, alias
Silicon Valley North. As Brian is wont to say, "Loose Lips Sink Chips.")

And do not become mean-spirited. Spreading the rumour that the in
place to party is the Trinidad/Tobago Embassy, "where *everyone* who
is *anyone*" goes, is particularly odious. It's a two-man embassy.

We *told* you times were rough.

Where to Eat in Ottawa

In our capital city it is important to eat, to be seen, and to be seen eating.
The upwardly mobile do *not* dine on Kraft dinner, Colonel Sanders'
finger-lickin' chicken, or McDonalds (no matter how many billions have
been served). Nor do they imbibe four-litre plastic containers of Quebec off-red.

Now we know that, for most of its history, Ottawa could have been
described as the gourmet's despair. Eating-wise it was Nothingsville.
The solution was always the same: go to Hull!

But times have been a-changing, and, over the last few years, so has the
Ottawa lifestyle. There has been an amazing proliferation of trendy
(English-type) pubs, restaurants (ethnic and otherwise), and new hotels.
Trendiest of all is the refurbished and reincarnated Byward Market,
packed with flowers, music, and merry places to eat and drink, with the
Rideau Street Development and the new Eaton Centre lying just above
it. Hull, of course, has retained its original trendy (French) flavour, but
some new and exciting eat-and-be-seen-in places have been added.
Here are just a few suggestions:

  In Ottawa:
  The Canadian Grill, Château Laurier (dull, but traditional.
  Now closed for renovations, probably in preparation for Our
  Coming)
  Tiffany's (splendid Victorian décor)
  The Casablanca (Moroccan and exotic)
  The Four Seasons Hotel (both bars and restaurants)
  The Westin Hotel (new, and in the Eaton Centre)

Stoney Mondays (singles' bar — fun, eh? — in the Market)

In Hull:
Pied du Cochon
L'Orée du Bois
L'Echelle de Jacob

In Kanata:
Silicon Fish and Chips

What Tories Should Drink (*alias* The Right Stiff)

Add, with or without a dash of bitters, this supplement to your drinking lexicon: Power Drinking, or Imbibing the Right Stuff.

This is not to say that drinking makes the political world go around — or at least until you keel over. In fact, showing up for standing committees of the House the day after sporting rug-burns on your nose is deemed bootless at best. Unless, of course, the burns were from a discreet meeting with a Khilim rug, the result of being overserved and understimulated.

Look, fellows: be temperate in your consumption. We stand on guard for thee, and we hope *you* will, too. In Ottawa, drinking is either self-destructive or heroic. Veteran politicians of the Ottawa triathlon — hard liquor, cocktails, and beer — insist you are what you drink. And since we are over 66% liquid already, what the hell.

But let's get back to those two sides of drinking: holding forth with a fifth is heroic, not to mention higher math; holding the floor as a stiff is self-destructive. Only a biopsy on your liver should tipple off your fellows that you were a true *magnum cum loud* of the Mickey Finnishing School of Hard Hops.

So, to help you along with How to Fit In With The Blue Crowd who now run Ottawa, here is a compendium of the Right Drinks:

Scotch: Neat. The spirit of Ontario/Alberta; scotches all rumours of wimpdom. As we tend to say after five or six too many, *Scotch, wa-hey!* Eh?

Bottled Water from Regina: More impressively potent than absinthe and/or applejack. This is the only drink in captivity that can be chewed. This stuff is so strong, we're surprised it doesn't dissolve the bottles it comes in. You can win the West with this. But at what cost? It's not expensive, but the liver transplant *is*.

Skreech: You may think you're scraping the bottom of the barrel with this brew. And you're right. But don't worry, you won't be thinking for long. Imbibing this impresses the Maritimers, or at least those who are still sober enough to be impressed. But *be careful*: You may awake to the sober notion that you signed away the offshore oil rights — and won't even care that you did.

Applejack — or *Le Gag d'Aviation*: Separates *les hommes* from *les anglais*, which just might be playing into the hands of the *Séparatistes*. A nasty beverage, to use the word very loosely. Sip *slowly*. If René begins to make sense, you've had enough. If the words ''sovereignty association'' seem perfectly logical to you, you've had far too much. If Robert Bourassa starts looking like the saviour of Quebec, you require copious amounts of Turkish coffee. If Brian seems decisive, keep drinking; you're okay.

The Right Cocktails (*not* The Right *Coat*-tails; Brian provided those, in the last election)

As Scotch is regarded as the power MBA intoxicant, cocktails are looked on as the MFA (Master of Fine Arts) libation. Cocktails are hooch with a party dress on. Or spats, if you wish. That notwithstanding, be on your guard. These are dangerous fireworks, and Victoria Day comes only once a year, remember! Try to avoid any drinks that arrive from the barkeep with little umbrellas.

—Spurn any concoction that appears to contain a hat once belonging to Carmen Miranda.

—Eschew any *spiritus frumenti* that resembles the flag of a Third World nation.

"But that's so negative!" you cry.
"A man's gotta drink!"
True. Which is why we now list some which you *should* favour, for your mind and liver, and not necessarily in that order:

The Bloody Mila:
1) Place ice-cubes in large glass.
2) Pour in two fingers of vodka (no relation to one finger of Trudeau).
3) Fill glass half-way with V-8 juice.
4) Season with the "Mila Mix" which you each received after your election to the House of Commons: onions, garlic, Hungarian paprika, hot red peppers, black pepper, hot chilli peppers, tabasco peppers, Dr. Peppers, salt and peppers.
5) Add wedge of lime; stir and drink very quickly. Keep passport on hand.

Zagreb Stinger:
Shake with ¾ cup of finely crushed ice:
1) 1½ jiggers of white *crème de menthe*.
2) 6 jiggers plum brandy.
3) Add "Mila Mix".
4) ½ jigger lime juice.
   Strain into chilled glasses and mouth.

Old-Fashioned Milahattan:
Put into an Old-Fashioned glass, and stir:
1) ½ teaspoon sugar syrup.
2) 2 dashes angostura bitters.
3) 1 teaspoon water.
4) Mila Mix to flavour.
Add: 2 ice-cubes, bourbon, or rye. Stir. Decorate with a twist of lemon peel, a thin slice of orange and a maraschino cherry.

Drink this one often enough, and you'll become so old-fashioned you'll be buying Kaiser-Fraser futures and John Crosbie's economics.

As all of these cocktails have a Yugoslavian touch to them, we must relieve any anxiety you have after ingesting any or all of the above, such as seeing things spotty and in black and white.

Fret no more. It's just the Dalmatia in you.

Martinis:
We hesitate to include this recipe because it is, no doubt, a mainly Grit invention. But since it has been an Ottawa standby for more years than we care to remember, we felt we should at least provide the basic ingredients:
1) Three to six ounces of gin (*not* vodka!).
2) Dry vermouth passed very lightly over the above. Served on the rocks or straight up.
3) An olive (Diefenbaker) for garnish.
Note: The plant *Dieffenbachia* can also render you speechless.

And, as we say in Tory circles:
Skol!
You Can Count on the Commerce!
Beggar Your Neighbours!
Here's to the Pin-Stripe, and Blue!
Chin Up!
To the Man in the Iron (Ore) Mask!
If You're Pink, You Stink! If You're Red, You're Dead! If You're Blue, You're *True*!
Here's Chin in Your Eye!
Let He Who Is Without Chin Cast the First Vote! (etc.)

What's In and What's Out

No, we are *not* referring to "the old in and out" from *Clockwork Orange*, which is a vulgarism we'd prefer Tories to avoid.

The Mulroney-Style Accessories

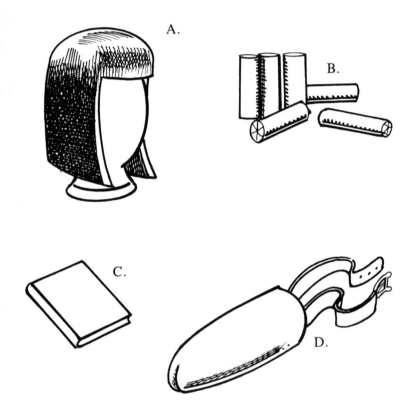

A.

B.

C.

D.

A. Mila hair-pieces—mandatory wigs come in two designer
      colours:
      Mila brown
      Tory blue rinse.

B. Rolls of spare change for:
  (a) pay phones.
  (b) cigarette machines.
  (c) Grits out of office.

C. Telephone Directory:
    Contents: (a) Business cronies. (c) Business cronies.
               (b) Business cronies. (d) Decorators.

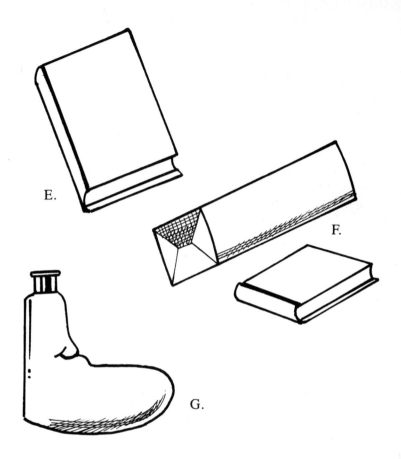

E.

F.

G.

D. Strap-On Chin: You new Tories will have to keep in shape. If wearing one of these seems odd, think about those guys with *double* chins.

E. Girls, here are words for you and Mila to live by, all conveniently contained in a handy, slender, easy-to-carry book. The book? *The Wit and Wisdom of Phyllis Schlafly*.

F. A half-day supply of Du Mauriers and a guide book of Parliament Hill, showing good hide-outs for sneaking a smoke.

G. Brian's Song cologne — who will be able to resist the sweet smell of success?

We mean the simple fact that things are going to change around Ottawa, now that the Good Guys are finally back on top. To assist you in knowing exactly what is acceptable — in personalities, clothes, styles, and culture — we present this important list.

Use it carefully. Memorize it. Then burn this page. (Removing it from the book first, please.)

In	Out
John Diefenbaker stories	Joe Clark references
The National Review	*The Toronto Star*
Florida vacations	Cuban vacations
chin	chinless
Ritz Hotel, Montreal	Winston's restaurant, Toronto
Mila	Maureen
Republicans	Democrats
Margaret Thatcher	Fidel Castro
gas hikes in gallons	gas hikes in litres
MOR (EZ Listening)	CBC
Baie Comeau	Schefferville
simp	wimp
VD	AIDS
The A–Team	*The Journal*
The Ottawa Citizen	*The Ottawa Citizen*
Richard J. Needham	Stephen Lewis
the colour blue	the colour red
Canadian Imperial Bank of Commerce	Royal Bank
Clint Eastwood	Ed Asner
Sunday Herald (so far not bad)	Sunday with Harold (your leftist cousin)
talcum powder	cocaine
baseball	squash
Chivas Regal	Teacher's
changing your name to his	keeping your own name
capital punishment	capital expenditures
Anne Murray	Nancy White
sushi bars	Chinese food
One Canada	A Community of Communities

Mila-Style (Reactionary Chic)

After years of shrugs and garter belts, we finally have one of the few instances wherein style and substance actually meet and shake hands in Ottawa.

And, my dears, let me tell you, it's Mowinckel this season! Giovanni Mowinckel! (Mila's decorator, dummy.) Tear up that advertising flyer for René of Smith Falls (Painting, Papering, Plumbing, and Pest Control a Specialty). No, you will no longer require the services of Hugo of Brandon (''We Know ReNo'' his motto). Throw away the card of Henri of Hull (''*Vous avez le cash*; *nous faisons le splash*.'')

And if Giovanni hasn't the time to do *you*, as he so brilliantly practised on Stornoway during the brief fling Brian and Mila had there, then consider — and *only* consider — decorators whose names suggest the pedigree of a Swiss mongrel: Horst Fantucci; Enrico Balthazar; André McBubbles; Jean Birch (of ''*Société*'' fame).

Mila and Mowinckel have brought Canada the Re-Generation. Reactionary chic. It's hep, baby. It is *today*, which is *yesterday*.

What do we *mean* by re-generation? Like Brian's politics, it's *simple*: Reacquaint. Readjust. Reaffirm. Realign. Reappoint. Reappraise. Reawaken. Rebuild. Re-cover. Redesign. Redecorate. Re-emerge. Re-educate. Re-establish. Refashion. Reunite. Revitalize. Renegotiate. Refinance. Regurgitate. Etc.

My dears, check into Mila make-overs. You know, you have to make the *Right* impression. And believe us when we reassure you that the results will not be la-de-da-tory, but *laudatory*.

Reactionary chic is not only decorating, but decor-living. So, for your edification and delightenment, we offer you a list of Ins and Outs to help you understand what we mean. No more Grit for the mill, here in Ottawa, but rather Tory for Glory.

In	Out

AT HOME FRIES

Cordon Bleu, chef	Frozen foods

MILA WEAR

Eddie Bauer and L.L. Bean for sportswear	drip-dry clothes Daniel Hechter
Giorgio Armani, Perry Ellis, Yves Saint-Laurent, size 8 gadabouts	Sergio Valente

BETTER HOMES & JARDINS

gardeners	power mowers
pergola	patio furniture
afternoon tea	kaffeeklatsch
tasties	happy hour

READY-WHEN-YOU-ARE ARCHITECTURAL DIGEST DECORATOR FLOWERS

Châteaugay day lilies forget-me-nots	plastic daisy decals

I-DON'T-KNOW-MUCH- ABOUT-ART-BUT-MY-DECORATOR- SURE-DOES — PART I: SCULPTURE

works by Sorel Etrog, Gerald Gladstone, Bill Reid	Toby mugs and jugs curling trophies
Inuit sculpture by Solomon Tegoklerrak	Legion chug-a-lug championship mug
slag memento from Iron Ore of Canada	

In	Out

I-DON'T-KNOW-MUCH-ABOUT-ART-BUT-MY-DECORATOR-SURE-DOES — PART II: WALL ART

In	Out
Works by Alex Colville, Jean-Paul Lemieux, Andy Warhol *originals* (or at least with numbers under 2,000) of Karen Kain selling Colgate toothpaste with Ross Petty	macramé wall hangings Franklin Mint plates featuring Norman Rockwell illustrations of a little girl lighting up her first cigar behind a barn LeRoi Neiman mechanical litho prints of World Hockey Association players Any works by Joyce Wieland (remember how Maggie felt about *Reason Over Passion*!)

LEAVE-IN-PLAIN-VIEW-DECORATOR BOOKS, AND AUTHORS

In	Out
Leonard Cohen's stuff, but the religious, not the sexy *The One-Minute Manager* *Leo Buscaglia: Collected, With Love, Love, Love* Limited Edition	The collected works of Richard Rohmer The collected works of Judith Krantz *Leo Buscaglia: Collected, With Love, Love, Love*

THERE'S-MORE-TO-IT-PHILOSOPHICALLY-SPEAKING: CHILDREN'S BOOKS

In	Out
Cinderella (Walt Disney version)	*Peter Pan* (Walt Disney version)

In	Out

IF-ONLY-WE-HAD-THE-TIME: TV RELAXATION

In	Out
Mary Tyler Moore reruns	Archie Bunker reruns
Star Wars	*Donkey Kong*
Zaxxon	*Frogger*

IF-ONLY-WE-HAD-THE-TIME: CINEMA

In	Out
More films like	Fewer films like
Moscow on the Hudson	*The Big Chill*

POWER PARTICIPACTION

In	Out
marathon jogging	softball
wild-game hunting	basketball

POWER SNACKING

In	Out
Mila Munchies:	chilli
caviar over oysters, or	grilled meat
spooned into baked pota-	burgers
toes with melted butter, a	*quiche lorraine*
dollop of *crème fraîche*,	white wine spritzers
and a sprinkling of minced	casseroles
green onion	canapés as French food
truffles, black or white	
sushi and cold pasta salad	

POWER ATTITUDES

In	Out
traditional	macho
us	them
upwardly mobile	downscale
savoir-flare	*savoir-faire*

In	Out

FABULOUS FURNITURE

In	Out
chintz, classic, elegant collections of appointments and accessories which co-ordinate beautifully with each other. It's *more* than a look. It's a *feeling*. But it's *more* than just a feeling! It's — well, we architecturally digress	Naugahyde anything that you sit or rest your feet or elbows on any living-room setting that smacks of south of the the bordello dinette or bankette, forget it! linoleum Arborite toppings bombasine upholstery

PAINT-CAN

plum's the word, m'dear	white-painted walls

Study this chapter carefully. You have everything to gain, and only gaucheness to lose. Impress one, impress all, with your *own* "Mila and Mowinckel show". You'll be pleasantly surprised and delighted by the Pivnickian response.

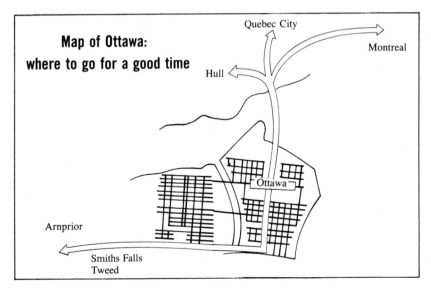

Map of Ottawa:
where to go for a good time

Quebec City

Montreal

Hull

Ottawa

Arnprior

Smiths Falls
Tweed

CHAPTER THREE

What Every Young Tory Must Know

Qs and As for Newly Elected MPs (For First-Timers Only, We Hope!)

We've already welcomed you to Ottawa, and suggested how to dress, where to stay, how to act. But there is something nearly as important, and that is the reason why you are here. (To be perfectly frank, it is something Brian likes to avoid, since it puts him permanently on record. Why *else* would anyone wish to come to Ottawa, except to make a living as an MP?)

You are here, as you may have forgotten since the election, because your constituents have chosen you to represent them. True, they may despise you, and may have voted for you only in order to get rid of the hated Grits, but that's okay too; you *were* elected, and you *are* here, and safe, for the next four to five years, and that is the important thing.

But what are your duties? Your responsibilities? What *is* government, anyway? And where do *you* fit in (aside from sitting on the Government benches, which is three-quarters of the battle, already)?

We have sat down with some of the finest legal and political minds in the country, a percentage of them Tories, and gathered together a list of Questions which you would most likely ask, and Answers to those Questions. And remember: even John Diefenbaker was once a beginning MP, no matter how hard you may find that to believe. Heck, our own *Brian* had never even held *elective office* before last fall! (We're still trying to figure out how he rose so high, *without* having ever been elected to anything. We think there may be a moral in here, somewhere.)

Anyway, to the questions at hand. Now remember: these are *not* all-inclusive; should you have any more, just call 995-WHAT in Ottawa (area code 613) for a quick A to any Q you may have.

Q. WHAT DO WE MEAN BY GOVERNMENT, ANYWAY?
A. Government can mean many things to many different people. How does one build roads? Keep them cleared of the damned snow? Keep the cops vigilant? Provide French services for the 2% of those in the Northwest Territories who rightfully demand them? Protect our great land from foreign invaders? (Something which no one has apparently worried about, before this election: see Chapter Six.)

The answer, of course, is Tory government: Us. Preferably elected by the People. Although we may have to resort to martial law, if that proves the only way to break the back of the Grits. Furthermore, without government, there would be no patronage, and without patronage, life would not be worth living.

Q. WHAT IS GOVERNMENT TO A NEWLY ELECTED TORY?
A. A well-paying job until the next election.

Q. WHEN IS THE NEXT ELECTION?
A. Don't panic. As we just *told* you, it could be as long as four to five years if we play our cards right, or if we at least keep our cards hidden. It is more than conceivable that you could be in Rockcliffe by 1988, on Easy Street by 1993, and in the Senate by 2000, at which point you need never worry about unemployment, meeting your mortgage, or being bugged by your damned constituents ever again.

Q. WHAT KIND OF GOVERNMENT DO WE HAVE IN THIS COUNTRY?
A. Kindness has nothing to do with it. We are *Tories*, not bleeding-heart liberals or socialists.

Q. NO, *REALLY*.

A. Well, some would say Canada has a parliamentary government, because men (and even some women) like you have a major say in running this frozen ranch. Others would call it a monarchy because the Queen (you know, the mother-in-law of Lady Di) is purportedly the source of authority in Canada. She once was, before the Grits whittled Her down.

Others might call it a democracy, since the people rule, but since they have finally re-elected *us* you don't have to worry about them until 1988 or 1989, at the earliest. And, to be frank, we really are a Government by Cabinet Minister, which is why you'd better be on Brian's good side if you *really* want the perks.

Q. WHAT IS CANADA'S CONSTITUTION?

A. Run-down, frail, weak. Until very recently — there's been a lot of talk about it in the papers and on TV. It's hard to believe but, until 1982, we actually had to get along with the BNA (Better Not Ask) Act of 1867, which was rather outmoded by this decade. Finally, barely two years ago we got The Canada Act, which includes a Charter of Rights and Freedoms, which, at the time of this writing, is too recent to have any real impact on our lives. So, if we *have* to use the War Measures Act in the near future, for instance, it'll probably still be okay.

Q. HAS OUR ENVIRONMENT SHAPED OUR POLITICAL SYSTEM?

A. You bet. First, the country is so darned *big*, making communication difficult until the left-wing CBC began its evil machinations back in the thirties. Secondly, we are made up of different cultures: mainly English, Scottish, Irish. And French. There are also large numbers of Germans, Poles, Scandinavians, Chinese, Italians, Ukrainians, Portuguese, Vietnamese, Japanese, an assorted black community, and so on. Some of these people settled here very early, some much, much later. But never forget, no matter what language they speak, they are *people*! And people *vote*! (See Chapter Seven.) Thirdly, we have a wretched climate which has led to the political cold shoulder, the political brush-off, and the Frosty Friday.

Q. HOW DO THE DESIRES OF THE PEOPLE REACH PARLIAMENT?

A. Through TV, radio, magazines, newspapers, lobbying, beseeching, prayer, pay-offs, and, most terrifying, through federal elections, like the Glory of 1984, and the Horror of 1980, which we'd rather not talk about. Usually, the people's demands reach government in one of the following three ways: overland, by way of Paraguay; on deaf ears; and quite easily, if you are black (especially Conrad or Montegu).

Q. HOW DO GOVERNMENTS RESPOND TO THE DEMANDS OF THE PEOPLE?

A. Like a mega-oil tanker turning, at full speed, on a dime.

Q. WHO CAN VOTE?

A. Of course. Joe Clark is well over the age of majority, even though he looks far younger.

Q. CAN WOMEN VOTE?

A. Yes. (For more information on this unavoidable subject, see Chapter Four, and Chapter Eight.)

Q. ARE ALL VOTES EQUAL?

A. As equal as nature intended. For example, note the ratio of men to women in government. Now why would you ask a cynical question like that?

Q. I'M SORRY.

A. That's not a question.

Q. IN CANADA, DOES THE MAJORITY RULE?

A. Yes and no. Sometimes as many as 60% of the voters in a riding may vote for one of the other two candidates, and the sneaky Liberal may slip through into office. Then again, as many as 65% of the voters in another riding may foolishly vote for one of the two other candidates, and the Progressive Conservative may wisely and cleverly slip through into office. So it swings both ways, if you'll pardon the expression.

But most of the time, the majority *does* rule, at least in open and closure situations.

Q. HOW ARE ELECTIONS HELD?
A. Snugly, in back pockets. And, in any case, when the polls are up, and open, respectively.

Q. WHO CAN RUN?
A. Joe Clark has the nomination in Yellowhead, and has every intention of running as far as he can. Brian welcomes him into the backbenches with open chin.

Q. WHO DOES RUN?
A. As you can see from the records, practically everybody. But mainly anyone who hasn't yet been appointed Queen's Counsel, and still feels the need for personal, if not financial, rewards.

Q. WHAT DOES A POLITICAL PARTY STAND FOR?
A. As little as possible, at least until it gets into office. We don't want the Grits to steal all our great ideas, now, do we? Actually, we won't stand for very much guff either — except in Question Period, where we're expected to let it all hang out, so to speak. And we don't mean exhibitionism, either.

Q. HOW ARE POLITICAL PARTIES ORGANIZED?
A. Surprisingly, there is a simple logic to it all. This is basically how it is done. First, straws are drawn.
1) Short straw I takes orders for sandwiches.
2) Short straw II prepares the Julio Iglesias and Diane Tell party tapes —make sure there is a sufficiently long extension cord for the recorder.
3) Short straw III makes certain that men and women observe the strict Tory party protocol: men against one side of the room; girls against the other.
4) Short straw IV, the party wit, will do a stand-up routine of Eugene Whelan impersonating Eugene Whelan.
(Sample Jokes: Eugene Whelan is so confident of someday residing in 24 Sussex Drive that he has already got the linoleum all picked out. The only tax that Gene has ever cut is syntax. Gene says he is the most famous politician in the world, and he may be right; Gaddafi was recently seen wearing a Eugene Whelan T-Shirt to a Press Conference. Etc.)

MP Office Guide

Basic Back-bencher

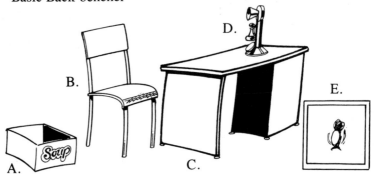

Basic Back-bencher
A. Filing cabinet — Libby's, Campbell's, Aylmer's, Jordan wine cartons.
B. Church-basement issue chair.
C. One metal desk. Drawers hard to open if more than three pieces of paper contained therein.
D. Telephone, *circa* 1926—it is reputed that the user can dial up Mackenzie King's mother. Unfortunately, this comes without an outside line.
E. Inuit print of Ookpik, machine litho'd, off register. Regarded as instant-teller withdrawal at the Art Bank.

Parliamentary Standing Committee Appointees:
As above, but without the telephone.

Parliamentary Secretary:
As above, but with the telephone, an office window, and a chair with arms.

MP Office Guide

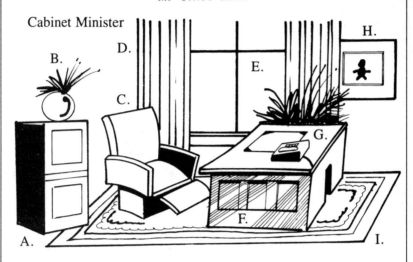

Cabinet Minister

Cabinet Minister
A. Deep filing cabinet.
B. Decorator plant (see Mila Style).
C. Executive jet chair.
D. Curtains. Real status symbol. You're so powerful you can snub your view.
E. A window looking out not on a pillar or wall.
F. Napoleon's desk, or facsimile.
   Duplessis' desk, or facsimile.
   W.A.C. Bennett's desk, or facsimile.
G. 12-line intercom — still no outside telephone line, but by choice.
H. West Coast Haida Raven print, off register.
I. Real status — Khilim rug over the indoor-outdoor wall-to-wall carpeting.

Q. HOW ARE POLITICAL PARTIES FINANCED?
A. Next question?

Q. SHOULD THERE BE FINANCIAL REFORM?
A. What are you, some kind of commie? A mole from the NDP?

Q. HOW IMPORTANT IS A PARTY LEADER TO A CANADIAN POLITICAL PARTY?
A. How important is a deity to a religion? How important is Wayne Gretzky to the Oilers? How important is an ovum to conception?

Q. WHY DO YOU ANSWER MY QUESTIONS WITH QUESTIONS? ARE YOU JEWISH?
A. Bite your tongue. The Canadian Embassy is *staying* in Tel Aviv, and that's *it*.

Q. SO ANSWER MY QUESTION ALREADY. JUST HOW IMPORTANT *IS* A PARTY LEADER?
A. Someone has to start the conga line. It's important. Someone has to organize the Trivial Pursuit teams. It's very important. Someone has to sort out who belongs to whom, and to which Volvo wagon, Honda Accord, Toyota Celica. It is *very* important. It's what develops party loyalty and party faithfuls.

Q. THOSE WERE ALL FOREIGN CARS.
A. We are for quotas only to a point. Next question.

Q. WHAT ARE GOOD LEADERSHIP QUALITIES?
A. We should tell you, and then you'll steal all Brian's great ideas? Just watch Brian carefully, make notes, and when he is in his early seventies start *considering* a run for it. *Not before.* Brian doesn't want to happen to *him* what happened to poor Joe.

Q. JUST WHO MAKES THE LAWS IN THIS COUNTRY?
A. Vested interests, although they occasionally wear two-piece suits. To be brutally frank, it's the Cabinet Ministers who make the laws, with the back-benchers nodding happily, the Senate rubber-stamping, and the RCMP turning a blind eye.

Q. WHAT GIVES THE CABINET SO MUCH POWER?
A. Brian, obviously. But there is more to it than that. The Cabinet is just a quick phone call away from the Man With His Finger on the Button, down in Washington, but it's more, still, than that. (What could be more powerful than nuclear war? Just keep on reading). You see, the Cabinet is truly the executive of the country, holding the reins on the massive Tory majority in Parliament. And it is the Cabinet that decides that *your* Newfoundland riding gets that new international airport: that *your* northern Saskatchewan riding gets that new ocean port; that *your* southern Ontario riding gets that new hospital, with the huge runway and ocean port around the back.

It's Power, pure and simple (*en français, pur et simple*); the Power that comes from wrestling inflation to the ground, tackling issues head-on; grappling with weighty concerns, and the thrust and parry of debate. Can you blame us for having so much Power, when we're in such great shape??

Q. WHAT DOES THE CABINET DO?
A. One could well ask WHAT *DOESN'T* THE CABINET DO, since it would take less time to answer! (A little hyperbole, there.)

For one thing, each member of the Cabinet must skilfully defend the position of his/her Deputy Minister. When this is inconvenient, each Cabinet Minister must be quick to fire that Deputy Minister (recall Bussières's deft handling of his problems last spring, over at Revenue).

More important, each Cabinet Minister is expected to truly go above and beyond the calls of duty, and pose for and with back-benchers in party brochures.

Even more important, each Cabinet Minister must cut ribbons, open arenas, fly first class, shake hands, shake heads (but more often than not, *nod* heads), and, when in trouble, crack heads.

Most important of all, a Cabinet Minister must and should reward his friends. Yes, it's a busy life, but a rewarding one. Remember that drunken gym teacher, back in junior high, who let you get away with murder in class? Get him a job with a Liquor Control Board. Your sister's husband is out of work? No longer, with the ins *you* have with half a dozen Crown

Corporations. There are literally thousands of other examples; you probably don't need our suggestions.

One last thing: As Cabinet Minister, you are expected to appear as a tight-lipped, steadfast good brick. What better analogy to illustrate Cabinet solidarity?

Q. IS A CANADIAN SENATE NECESSARY?
A. Do children need candy? Do cars need chrome? Does your wife need a new dress? As King Lear says, "O reason not the need!" You may not *appear* to need those things to survive, but how much better life is with that candy, that chrome, and that new dress!

But enough of waxing poetic! To the point: of course we need the Senate. It's the arena of sober second thought on contentious legislation (although the word "sober" is a foreign one to most Senators, and absolutely none of them had a "second thought" about accepting Cash For Life).

Why, many a thoughtful addendum has been contributed during a rousing Senate debate, awakening opinions (and Senators); ringing the alarm regarding worrisome legislative passages; stretching those areas into which "fairness" needs to be imposed; shaking free from the suffocating red tape imposed by law and in the legislative process . . . one could go on and on! To be honest, the Canadian Senate is the stuff that dreams are made of!

Not only that; do you realize what it would cost Parliament to actually build a *new* senior citizens' home in such a prime location?

Q. HOW NECESSARY IS THE POST OF GOVERNOR-GENERAL?
A. Slightly less than the Senate; see above.

Q. THEN WHY DO WE HAVE ONE?
A. Don't be cynical. We have *one* because two or more Governors-General would simply be cost-prohibitive. Furthermore, it is merely a figurehead appointment, with no real powers — much like the Vice-president of the United States, the President of the State of Israel, and Ed Broadbent. Still and all, a figurehead is a figurehead, and one must admit that Madame Jeanne Sauvé possesses both the figure and the head for the job.

Q. WHAT DOES THE CIVIL SERVICE DO?
A. Is there a time-limit on this question?

Q. LOOK WHO'S BEING CYNICAL! OKAY, LET ME TRY AN-
OTHER. DO WE HAVE A FEDERAL SYSTEM OF GOVERN-
MENT, AND WHY?
A. Which would you prefer: making a federal case out of something,
or being thought of as a provincial person? You and I both know the
answer to that one.

The history of this goes way back. John A. Macdonald toasted the federal system, drank to it, downed his pride, kept his spirits up, scraped
the dregs of the provincial system, and brimmed with pride at his success.
You want more proof than that?

Q. IS IT POSSIBLE TO CHANGE THE SYSTEM?
A. Sure. Vote Republican.

Q. I DON'T UNDERSTAND WHAT YOU MEAN.
A. Perhaps we should explain this more fully.

Often, cynical Canadians will ask an absurd question like "What's
the difference between you Conservatives and the Republicans in the
States?" But even stupid questions deserve good answers, so here are a
few which you may wish to use:

   —the Tories rule Ottawa, whereas the Republicans rule Washington.

   — Brian is much younger than Ronnie, and Brian doesn't dye
his hair.

   — Mila has much longer, more fashionable hair than Nancy
Reagan.

   — the Republicans wouldn't think of testing Cruise missiles
over their own territory, whereas we *would*, and *do*.

   — the Republicans swore that the budget deficit was far too
high at $50 billion, and they managed to get it down to $218

billion. We Tories believe that the Canadian budget deficit of over $30 billion is far too high, and we hope to get it down as well.

— the Republicans can only rule with the same leader for two terms, eight years in total; we Tories can rule Canada for the next fifty years under Brian, please God.

— the Republicans believe in Voodoo Economics, whereas we Tories believe in Reaganomics.

— the Republicans mine El Salvador, whereas we sell deadly airplanes to the Germans.

— the Republicans are slowly trying to put an end to acid rain, whereas we Tories are fighting to have the Republicans quickly put an end to acid rain.

— the Republicans appear to be utterly unconcerned about the blacks of the United States, who number over 10% of the total population, whereas there are far fewer blacks in Canada, and they're mainly from the Caribbean, anyway.

— the Republicans fear socialism, whereas we Tories just ignore it.

— the Republicans rescue companies like Chrysler, which roar back in wild success, whereas we Tories rescue companies like Dome and Canadair and de Havilland, which can barely squeak.

— Reagan left Hollywood and came to Washington to "make it", whereas most Canadians, Tories included, feel that they have to *go* to Hollywood to make it.

— Republicans go to Palm Springs for vacations; Tories go to Florida (but not Cuba where Republicans wouldn't be caught dead, and probably would end up dead if they *were* caught).

Is that enough ammunition for you?

Q. WHY IS QUEBEC ANY DIFFERENT FROM THE OTHER
PROVINCES?
A. You want the answer in French or English?

Q. ENGLISH.
A. We thought so. There's your answer in a nutshell.

Q. I DON'T UNDERSTAND.
A. *Pardonnez-moi?*

Q. *JE NE COMPREND PAS.*
A. Better. Keep it up, and maybe someone in the Province of Quebec
will condescend to explain it all to you.

Q. WHAT IS SOVEREIGNTY ASSOCIATION?
A. Even René Lévesque doesn't know, and he's fully bilingual. We
think it has something to do with "having your cake and eating it too"
but it loses something in the translation. Most things, come to think of
it, lose something in the translation, which is one of the big problems
we face in this country.

Q. HOW ARE PROVINCIAL GOVERNMENTS THE SAME AS
THE FEDERAL?
Q. For one thing, they tend to be led by Tory governments, which sug-
gests a certain intelligence, doesn't it? They also have a Lieutenant-
Governor who is powerless, a Premier and Cabinet who are all-powerful,
a legislative assembly which is worthless, and an electorate which is
worth even less.

In a nutshell, which is where most of them belong, provincial governments are to the federal what the lamprey is to the fish world.

Q. WHAT DO PROVINCIAL GOVERNMENTS DO, ASIDE FROM
ELECTING TORIES?
A. For this question, we need a chart:

PC GOVERNMENTS	GRIT GOVERNMENTS	NDP
wheedle	wheedle	get defeated
obfuscate	obfuscate	
cajole	cajole	
bitch	bitch	
rage	rage	
circumvent	circumvent	
toady	toady	

Q. WHY HAVE PROVINCIAL AND LOCAL GOVERNMENTS AT ALL?

A. We've been asking ourselves that question for years. Now that we're in power at last, maybe we can *do* something about it.

Q. WHAT IS THE RULE OF LAW?

A. Stand firm. Give anyone a centimetre and they'll take a metre. The Rule of Law refers to not raising one's hand, voice, or any other demonstrable device against one's betters or authority figures.

Q. HOW DOES THE CANADA ACT, 1982, PROTECT OUR FREEDOM?

A. Alas, it does not protect the freedom of Members of Parliament any more than the public, and it does, alas, protect the freedom of the public more than ever before. As of this writing, however, the Charter of Rights protects in the same manner, and to the same extent, as a flak jacket on a flea protects it from a bazooka.

Q. HOW LONG DID YOU SAY I CAN KEEP THIS CUSHY JOB, AGAIN?

A. You *are* insecure, aren't you? If you listen to Brian very carefully, and don't do stupid, dumb things (see *Discipline of Power: The Conservative Interlude and the Liberal Restoration*, remaindered at a bookstore near you, pages 3 through 363 especially), then you could be here in Ottawa, sitting pretty, for many, many years to come. Think Power. Think Pension. Think Perks. Think Senate. You may never have to work again.

How to Look and Act Busy

You are a public servant, even though you may not enjoy that image. (Not the public part; the idea of serving.) But you are, and your taxes are paid for by the little folk, and it is important that they feel they are getting their money's worth.

Which is why we have prepared this section, laying out a style and behaviour pattern learned only from careful observation of those in the higher echelons of big business and huge government.

The people who have the most expertise in looking and acting busy are usually those who have suffered (or gloried in) Lateral Promotion. They are men and women who have been shunted sideways in their careers, not rising, exactly, but not falling either. And they manage to maintain this amazing equilibrium through the tricks indicated below:

1) Rush to your desk.

2) Grab a folder, manila envelope or attaché case.

3) Stuff it full of paper; that morning's *Globe*, torn into legal-sized sheets, if desired.

4) Tear off your jacket.

5) Roll your sleeves half-way up your forearms.

6) Suck in your breath.

7) Walk briskly from Point A (your desk? the water-cooler? the picture window?), past all the important people in your office, to Point B, usually a washroom, or a hideaway behind the parliamentary cafeteria, or perhaps where the Mounties feed the horses.

8) Sit back and pull out a novel—Louis L'Amours are recommended — or maybe *How To Improve Your French*, which is always useful.

9) Read a few chapters; relax.

10) Loosen the knot of your tie; it makes it look as though you've been working up a sweat. (And you probably have; Ottawa can be like an oven in the late spring and early fall.)

11) Tousle your forelock, if you have one.

12) Tear back from Point B to Point A (see #7, above, and merely reverse).

13) Important: if anyone beckons to you when you are going in either direction, wave them brusquely off, as if whatever you are carrying in your folder/attaché case is far too important for you to stop.

14) Walk with great deliberation and determination, as if you were leaning into a force-eight gale.

15) You are back at your desk. You can take a break now; go to the water-cooler; lunch; whatever. Somehow, somewhere on your journey into nothingness, a photographer, perhaps a constituent from your riding, saw you walk with such determination, such deliberation. The word will get around: you are a Force to be Reckoned With; you are Cabinet Material; you are Senate Fodder. All this, and you move towards the point where the nurse gets the doctor, or your fluency in French improves. This is what it means to be a successful back-bencher. And if you keep it up, you won't be warming those benches for long. Bravo!

What to Do When in Doubt

Appoint a Royal Commission.

Obfuscation

by W.G.D., Himself, Premier

Many of you may think that obfuscation can lead to pimples on the hand, or blindness, but you are confused. Obfuscation is one of the cardinal rules of politics.The main point of obfuscation is to skirt around issues so much that Alfred Sung gets jealous. To be so slick in your answers, your words slide off the magnetic tape of the reporters. To be so roundabout in your replies, listeners reach for Gravol.

Some examples? It's simple. Let's say you are asked about the 45% unemployment rate in your riding. You answer "We are taking a hard look at the situation of the underemployed and those between jobs, and we think you won't be displeased by our conclusions." (By the time anyone thinks of asking when those conclusions might be forthcoming, or what they might be, you are well on your way to the next question.)

Another. You are challenged about daycare. Try: "If it weren't for children, Canada would have no future. And the fact that those children are *cared* for, whether at home, in the office, or in the alleys — or on the beaches, for that matter, when the weather is good enough — is central to the thinking of the Progressive Conservative Party right across this great land. Nor do we Tories stop at daycare. Why not nightcare? Why not care for the little tykes right around the clock? Canada's survival as a nation depends on our children, and the PCs pride themselves on being at the forefront of that concern."

Okay, let's do it as multiple choice. Here's a real toughie: abortion. Check off one as the ideal obfuscation, which will help you not only *get* votes, but, more important, not *lose* votes:

1) Abortion is a matter between a woman and her doctor.

2) Life begins at the moment of conception, making any abortion an act of murder.

3) When one confronts the perennial question of abortion, one has to balance, on one hand, the rights of the woman to control her own body, and, on the other, the rights of the unborn. The Progressive Conservatives do not take that balancing lightly, nor should any of our millions of citizens, whatever their religious, ethnic, or social backgrounds. A woman's body is precious; so is the developing fetus. One cannot inflict one's personal beliefs on womankind, or on the future infant. A complex issue indeed, and one which we Tories feel strongly about, one way or the other, and we will fight to the death for the right for every one of you, if you vote for us, to express your own feelings. Thank you very much.

Did you check #3? If so, then you have a good chance of being in power for many decades as well. Indeed, the last answer, taken directly from a major Tory address, led to ''Thanks for your support'' letters from both Cardinal Carter and Henry Morgentaler. Obfuscation is no crime; it is, in fact, the true way to political survival and progress.

From the Grits' Otto Lang to the Tories, Utter-Lang: Technospeak, Mandarinese, and Babble-Can

As anyone in CUSO or the diplomatic corps will gladly point out, you don't send a student or an official to the USSR without his (or, possibly, her) knowing Russian; to Greece without knowing Greek; to Angola without knowing Spanish (since the Cubans tend to insist upon it).

Well, you are in Ottawa for the next few years, and probably the next few decades. So you have some language study to do—not *only* in French, if you are English, and vice versa.

Unfortunately, Berlitz does *not* have a two-month total immersion course in these new languages we're about to discuss. Yet here you are in Ottawa, and you are probably already discovering that — whether Francophone or Anglophone — you are still not able to understand when you are spoken to, or to make yourself understood when you speak to others.

It's rather like being dropped, unprepared, into the heart of Beijing, able only to utter "Dim Sum". (Or, for that matter, like John Crosbie dropped, unprepared, into the middle of Sept Isles, able only to utter "Dim Sum".)

Let's begin with a smattering of techno-jargon. *Don't panic.* At first it will feel as though you've just been tossed into Hudson Bay on April the first. But just sort of ease yourself in, and don't recoil from it. Soon, to take the analogy further, you will become accustomed to the chill. Why, it won't be long before you are swimming like a fish! It will be as if you will have dove right in!

Bad grammar in that last sentence? Of course. But the first rule to learn about the official lexicon is that the noun "priority" can become a verb. Similarly all other grammatical structures and rules are also tossed to the wind. Got that? Okay, let's begin:

> **Core dumped:** In your concern for your fellow human beings, your heart is as generous as that of Idi Amin.

> **Gating event:** This is not a political fund-raiser. Instead, it indicates the necessity of choosing a direction when confronted by a fork in the road.

> **Interface:** To dialogue with. (We warned you about the grammar.)

> **To access:** This makes the heart grow fonder.

> **To format:** A system of non-thinking. A means for the thoughtless to manifest the unthinkable. Manifestly.

> **Windowing:** Juggling your priorized options all at once.

> **Interrupt-driven:** Not your 1975 Chev, but the normal run of official schizophrenia protracted by trying to please two political masters and satisfying neither.

Read-only memory: A neo-Luddite. Someone who'll never learn and learn good (like a Luddite should).

Programmable read-only memory: Someone who'll learn and learn good, learn good, learn good. (We *did* warn you about the grammar, grammar, grammar.)

Pushing things on the stack: This one just means "overwhelmed". But why use only one good word, when five not so good words can be essentialized?

Bandwidth: In no way connected with the phrase, "Who was that bandwidth Michael Jackson?" Rather, this alludes to the amount of information exchanged during an interfacing. We like to think of our bandwidth as broad and user-friendly, unlike the bandwidth achieved by investigators for Revenue Canada.

User-friendly: Not available at Revenue Canada. Sorry.

I'm down: Shut off. The sad fate of any electorate possessing a majority government, for up to five years, hopefully.

Menu: A list of what we Tories serve up — without prices, of course. (*Bien sûr.*)

Let us press on to Mandarinese and Babble-Can, which are often interchangeable, and most certainly user-friendly. Be warned, you may well be discouraged at first. But you will not *always* sound like a new French member speaking English (or even French, for that matter). Practise, and you'll soon be shining like the seat of a mandarin's pants:

Optimizing concerns: Breaking into a cold sweat, when, for example, the hoofbeats of a terrible Gallup are heard approaching in the distance.

Paucity of interface: As gregarious as former PM Trudeau was, to Tory back-benchers. Or to his *own* back-benchers. Or, for that matter, to his Cabinet.

Options priorized: A call for a Royal Commission on a sticky matter.

Counterweights and linkages: Inducements and persuasions.

Short Take-Off and Landing: Stall (for more money).

Dialogue with Canadians: Monologue to Canadians.

Entrench our paramountcy: Be prepared to get even the dead out to vote for us in the next election.

Lowbridged, or **rendered non-obstante:** The equivalent of being appointed High Commissioner to Churchill, Manitoba.

Beige Papers. White Papers. Orange Papers. Green Papers: Material on which messy problems appear. If you have ever been involved in training an incontinent puppy with newspapers, you will know precisely what to do with all *that*.

Government by Goldfarb: Indicating the speaker's belief that the Jews *do* run Ottawa. To be taken with a pillar of salt.

Double-Track, Two-Track: We'll make the trains run on time, on time.

Block-funding: Senate appointments and all the necessary Porky Piggery, accomplished at one go.

Tax Transfers: Just be sure to spell the federal minister's name right, (and his ministry's,) on Public Works signs.

East-West dialogue: Where talk is cheap, but can still cost a fortune in the end.

North-South dialogue: "I'm going to the Virgin Islands over the Christmas break; how about you?"

Special status and duality: Even we can't figure out this one. Any ideas?

Bilingualism: A politician fluent in both technospeak and Mandarinese.

Acronyms You Must Know:

CBC	CDC	CEO
BVD	STANFIELD'S	CFDC
CFTO	CIDA	COC
CTC	CUIO	DND
ECC	EMP	AIB
NFB	CCC	FBDB
FCCC	USSR	NATO
FIRA	FLORA	FAUNA
HWC	UIC	INA
ITC	XTC	MCC
MRC	NAC	NCC
NEB	NFB	TV
NMC	NPA	NRC
IBM	UAW	CIO
NTC	PCO	PMO
POW	PSC	PSSRB
RCMP	CIA	FBI
SC	SS	SSHRC
TB	VD	VA
AIDS	AGCAN	STATSCAN
TRANSPOCAN	CANCAN	CHACHACHA
LSD	NSF	CHIPS

It is not necessary to know what each of these acronyms stands for, really. It's what the public *thinks* they "stand for". Their value? They are like a Quaalude, popped at the proper moment. Sprinkle any one, or as many as you wish, right in the middle of your speeches, set up with this key phrase:

We intend to take a hard look at . . . (fill in with the acronym(s) of your choice).

The audience will infer from your impassioned declaration that you aim to cut back on department spending, when actually your "hard look" is simply a desperate attempt to remember what the hell the acronym(s) refer(s) to.

To quote a famous Tory journalist, have you apprehended the totality of your confusion?

Tory Fund-Raising Dinners

One of the greatest ways of raising funds for your political needs, not to mention bikes for the kids, is the fund-raising dinner. They can be fun, they can be entertaining, they give you the chance to get to know your constituents without having to answer too many embarrassing questions.

That said, there are some concerns regarding these fund-raisers, and you should know about them. Here are but a few:

— If your fund-raiser goes for a dollar a plate, then you are *no*where.

— If the chicken served is vulcanized, then you are *definitely* nowhere.

— If the most successful fund-raising dinner you've ever held is in Témiscaming, you are *positively* nowhere.

— If you are heckled during your thank-yous at your fund-raising dinner, then you may be in trouble.

— If there is sectarian violence during the appetizer course, then you know you're in trouble.

— If every table at your fund-raising dinner is crudely divided along linguistic, or religious, or racial lines, you are really in trouble.

— If, during the main course, someone leaps up and begins

screaming, "My tooth! I've broken my tooth!", you are in serious trouble.

— If, during the dessert, a large number of people fall over murmuring something about "toe-main", you are in debt in more ways than you may realize.

— If Stompin' Tom Connors plays the head table in, or out, and crashes through the plywood stage you provided for him to stomp on, you are miserably out of touch.

— If, during your remarks, people begin to screech, *"Parlez français!"* — and you *are* speaking French — you should panic.

— If, during your remarks, people begin to yell, "Quit speaking French!" and the only French you have used is *"Mesdames et messieurs"*, you should freak out.

— Have you considered garage sales? A mailing? There are lots of other possibilities from which you can raise needed cash. Phone 995-CASH (area code 613) for recommendations.

Being Careful (More Words to the Wise)

You are now a Public Figure, with all that this implies. Other people may cheat on their income tax; you will be scrutinized and caught. Other people may cheat on their wives; you will be seen doing it, and shamed. Other people may write letters to judges asking for favours, or pay off traffic cops; you, unless you are a Grit, will probably be brought to light and, eventually, to trial.

Call it unfair. Call it cruel. Call it nasty, brutal, and short. But call it Ottawa.

Now, where were we? Oh, yes: be careful. A few suggestions:

Things you should not back into: RCMP stake-outs
USSR cook-outs
bayonets

Things you may back into: the Senate
                                Brian's swimming pool

Remember: The best Tory politician is one whose obituary can be reported only on the Religion page.

As Brian always says: "Keep your chin clean."

Deviant Behaviour, Extra-Commons

You must consider this: A kiss could be amiss. A sigh could be a lie. The fundamental rules apply, as time goes by.

Look. You represent the highest calling this side of the Senate. Keep your nose clean, and in plain view.

Remain chary of dubious situations and portentous liaisons. It's one thing to give secrets to the Russians, assuming we have any of any value; it's quite another to give your heart, thoughts, or a more private part of your anatomy to a person of the other sex. (Whichever.)

Honourable Member refers *solely* to your presence in the House of Commons.

Do not let yourself be thought of as "He of the open fly and closed mind". Closed minds can go far in a Tory administration; open flies are too often likely to let the cat out of the bag, so to speak.

Gentlemen, leave the wearing of high heels, net stockings, and naughty French-Canadian lingerie to those in External Affairs, preferably on a lengthy and unpublicized trip to Boston's Combat Zone.

Ladies, kindly refrain from affecting monocles, riding crops, sensible brogues, and Bloomsbury suits. We'd be a lot happier if you left all that to Sports Canada or Studio D of the NFB.

Pay strict attention to the backgrounds of, shall we say, any surreptitious assignations of the extramarital kind. We are just as familiar as the next guy with the fact that two wives is bigamy and one wife is monotony. (The same applies, in reverse, to female MPs.) Nor are we so naive as to believe that nothing of this sort transpires.

But may we remind you of the cry of the assaulted MP during the Munsinger Affair: "Migawd! My Gerda is killing me!" *Don't let it happen to you!*

As for those of you who, heaven forbid, swing both ways, let us remind you of what happened to Oscar Wilde. Before your time? How about Billie Jean King? Too sporty for you? Try Boy George. True, he's making millions, but he's a rock star, not a parliamentarian.

A few sayings to pin up on your blackboard (and the *only* pin-ups you should have, we might add):

— Discretion is the Better Part of Amour.
— Government People Have No Place in Any Bedrooms of the Nation Except Their Own.
— No Extramarital Sex Please, We're Canadian.
— Love Thy Neighbour as Thyself, But Don't Screw Yourself.
— Read a Good Book Regularly, But Do Not Curl Up with a Page.

Bumper-Stickers for Tories: Possible Slogans

The Grits have Red Leaf Communications, don't they, starring Jerry Grafstein, Keith Davey, and others too awful to mention. Well, we have our *own* men, and they have been working hard on the kind of slogan which will really grab — and hold — the body politic, to coin a phrase.

The following have been considered over the past few months, and we would appreciate your input. We include some comments by either Brian or some of his closest advisers, about these gems of wisdom. If Ford can have a Better Idea, then we Tories can certainly come up with our own grabbers, which will live for ever in the hearts and minds of men. And girls, too. Personkind, in fact.

Come Work with Me!
(Note: Trudeau used it in 1968; surely we can be more original than this!)

The Land Is Strangled
(Too negative, although it has a nice ring to it)

Lead with your Chin
(Not bad)

Chin Up
(Not any better)

Brian's Buyin'
(It sounds too much like a pub. And aren't we out to convince the electorate that Mulroney and the Tories will spend *less* than the open-pocketed Grits?)

I Break for Tories
(A winner, but only for bumper-stickers; otherwise, it doesn't make much sense, except to break dancers, maybe)

Now More Than Ever
(Richard Nixon used this, and I think the NDP is now using it, come to think of it. We don't mind being hooked with Nixon, I think — but please, *not the NDP!*)

Less Progressive, More Conservative
(Marvellous. A winner!)

Mulroney and You!
(I'm really fearful that Ronald McDonald might sue. Better pass on this one)

We Have Nothing to Fear but FIRA Itself
(I love it. It seems to echo something else I heard in politics, but until I think of it, I say go with a few thousand buttons. Does anyone else remember what this one is playing on?)

Better Safe and Tory
(Too subtle. And the word "safe" makes me think of condoms, which could alienate the Catholic vote, which is *huge*)

Guns, Guts, and Tories
(Nice, if a little strong)

The Chin Stops Here
(Another winner)

Everything is Hunky-Tory!
(Delightful, but it could displease the Ukrainians, and we might lose Saskatchewan. Is it worth it?)

Being in Power Means Never Having to Say You're Tory
(Too literary. And Eric Segal could hit us with copyright infringement. Talk with our lawyers before acting on this one)

We Know the Pros and Cons
(A goodie, but the image of cons, as in ex-cons, could work against us)

He Kept Us Out of War
(But what if it isn't true?)

Make Manitoba Bilingual!
(Are you *crazy*?)

Make Ontario Bilingual!
(Which side are you *on*?)

CHAPTER FOUR

The Ps and Qs of Parliamentary Behaviour

Behaviour in the House (of Commons)

"Common" may usually mean "ordinary" or "vulgar", but not in the term "House of Commons".

The House of Commons is the main public arena. The Big Time. Where It All Happens. You will be observed from the public galleries, the press galleries, and on television. Because of all this scrutiny, we feel it is imperative that great caution be taken in order that the new MP make an excellent impression.

Dress Code
1) Buy and wear conservative Warren K. Cook or Samuelson suits, which are usually favoured by doctors and lawyers with blue-chip stock portfolios. (Underneath, Stanfield underwear is a *must*.) These suits may be purchased at E.R. Fisher, Holt Renfrew, Noël Kerr, Don Renaud, and other fine men's-wear shops in Ottawa.
2) Female MPs should consider Holt Renfrew (ladies' department, please), Eaton's, the Bay, and, for the more matronly, Ada Mackenzie (which is as good a Scottish name as we've ever heard, and probably Tory, to boot).
3) Avoid Canadian Tire Outdoor and Patio Wear.
4) Pass by the Kresge's Dollar Daze Sales.
5) Resist the ever-present temptation to experiment with plaids,

stripes, and luminous colours, especially simultaneously.

6) On television, unusual clashes of patterns and colours cause an electronic phenomenon known as "strobing". You could end up resembling Captain Kirk beaming down from the *Enterprise* but not molecularly regrouping. (We recall one Grit back-bencher whose apparel was of such cataclysmic disorder that his trappings caused static during the simultaneous translation.) So dress as if you are going to a funeral, and not as if you are about to read the local TV sports and weather in Cornerbrook.

What You Should Never Be Seen Doing

1) Reading a newspaper, or lying back in your Commons seat with the newspaper gently rising and falling over your face.
2) Selling provincial or federal lottery tickets to fellow MPs in the house.
3) Absentmindedly moving your fly up and down to the cadence of a speaker's voice.
4) Looking lean and hungry. See Shakespeare's (who was not Canadian) *Julius Caesar* (who might as well have been, considering the way he ended up, almost Tory-like). To be a successful Tory is really Darwin in action: the survival of the fattest.
5) Selling a used 1973 Buick convertible with white walls and wire wheels to the Prime Minister or any of his Cabinet Ministers during Question Period.

House Behaviour

1) You do not address the despised Opposition member in the way in which he may be accustomed (ex-con, crook, louse, scumbag, fruit, buffoon, etc.), but rather you address the Speaker of the House and, through him, the dishonourable member of the Opposition.

A typical declaration would be, "Mister Speaker, I beg to differ with the Honourable Member of Toronto North-east, in his absurd declaration about the new budget. . . ."

(NB: The new Speaker of the House is a male, so it is once again proper to say "Mister Speaker". For the past few years, Madame Jeanne Sauvé was speaker, making it necessary for House members to address "Madame Speaker". For the vast majority of the MPs, this was simply too difficult to accomplish. If you are one of the MPs who was in the House during the tenure of Madame Sauvé, you are herewith invited to continue using the phrase "Mister Speaker", and no longer feel guilty or foolish for saying it.)

2) Shake your fist a good deal, preferably into the camera.
3) Look exceedingly indignant, as though someone has just sold you a used 1973 Buick convertible in positively dreadful condition.
4) Keep mumbling, both under and over your breath, "Jobs! Jobs! Jobs!" It worked for Brian; it will also work for you.

Your Maiden Speech

We know how you feel. We went through it, too. Look at Brian — he had to start at the *top*, unprotected by rows of seats from the glare of cameras, lights, and public scrutiny.

You probably have a nightmare vision of what this event will be: the Commons is jammed to standing room only; the Speaker recognizes you from the Chair; the Commons' TV cameras zoom in on you, and you address the nation.

Your constituents watch in the Legion Hall over a few drafts of Hi-Life. And what will you say, after *your* few drafts — of your speech, that is? Will you singlehandedly bring on a Golden Age of parliamentary oratory? Or will you only be capable of mumbling a few ill-chosen words?

Relax!! That is *not* what will happen!

—First of all, no one will be in the House. A mere quorum; a skeleton crew.

— Those present will be up and down like a three-storey elevator, or Xaviera Hollander on a holiday weekend, conversing with colleagues, chatting with the pages, reading newspapers.

— The Speaker will recognize you, and then slip back into his seat, and semi-consciousness.

— You will not be shown on TV, as only Question Period is televised.

— As for your few speech drafts, forget it. The party has highly skilled and even more highly paid work-jockeys to handle your speechifying.

— Just read it and go back to sleep.

Now, most maiden speeches can be likened to Moses wandering forty years in the desert: dull, dull, dull! You will recall what De Mille did with the exodus from Egypt: he played up the Ten Plagues, the Splitting of the Red Sea, and the Receiving of the Ten Commandments. The wandering, after all, was the least interesting. Dig?

So, we here present a ghosted address which typifies how a professionally constructed maiden speech should read:

(The following should be delivered with poise and élan, but not so much poise and élan that it elicits cries of "Author! Author!" (There were, in fact, about a dozen author-authors.)

"Mr. Speaker, Honourable Members! I'm delighted to have this opportunity to speak to you about. . . .(Fill in your riding)

(Here the novice too often wanders off into a series of tangential bromides relating to his or her riding. But not *you*. Witness:)

"I could put the Honourable Members present into a comatose state by voicing the usual constituency softcore propaganda, but I feel there are far more pressing and urgent matters to extrapolate on."

(Here, some honourable, and some less than honourable, members will open one eye in your direction, expecting a harangue about local concerns.)

"I could unleash a torrent of lavender accusations over governmental misdeeds, misdemeanours, and miscreants, and launch lavender expletives at the honourable misanthropes missing or present. But I feel that *Beauchesne's Parliamentary Rules and Forms* (fifth edition) is not quite prepared to launch a sixth edition.''

(Some nervous but thankful chuckles and chortles from the handful of honourable members still awake or recently awoken.)

"However, Honourable Lounge Lizards — ''

(This abruptly awakens the Speaker, who quickly orders an apology from you, citing that Beauchesne's has ruled *out*, in its list of unparliamentary words, anything with the word "reptile" in it, or references to things reptilian. However, you have achieved an effect, an accomplishment usually unheard of in maiden speeches. You apologize and resume:)

"However, Honourable . . . *Members* . . . I wish to state, with all the conviction I can muster, that optimism disengaged from reality is dangerous!

"We could easily range from unbridled optimism to chaos, if we first discover the truth, and then *lie*! When the cost benefits deny our effortless superiority, we are in the ever-present danger of creating a Dickensian Bleak House — not in the mother country, but right here — in our fair and pleasant land!!

"*This* we will *never* do!!''

(You now have awakened those few who are actually present. This part of the speech is called "the Royal George". It is the oral equivalent of transcribing Handel's *Fireworks* into Muzak. In other words, it *sounds* as if it is all there, but if something is missing, they are too tranquillized to question. Now, the Big Finish:)

"Mr. Speaker, Honourable Members: the future is in our hands, and in the hands of our children, and their children's children. All hands must surely be placed on deck, assuming, quite rightly, that we are playing with a full one. Nor shall we ever, ever wash our hands of it.

"Thank you.''

(Sit down. You may now keep your mouth shut for the next four years.)

Congratulations. You are in *Hansard*.

Important Issues and Glib Answers for Same

Being a Member of Parliament is more than just running for office, hiring staff, repaying old debts, occasional visits to Ottawa and less occasional visits to your riding. It's a responsibility. A responsibility to *stand* for something.

People want you to choose sides. To have opinions. To possess views. Fortunately, most of those people are not relevant to your future: they are reporters, so-called journalists, lobbyists, those who live outside your riding. Troublemakers, in fact.

But on any number of issues, you *will* have to take a stand, and it is most important that your stand not be in conflict with that of your Leader. Which is where this all-important section comes in: what to think, feel, and, most crucial, to *say* about the various questions facing our country today. You may wish to stretch some of them a bit, which is why we occasionally give a few alternatives. But, in the main, what you see here is *what you should answer*.

Write these on your shirt cuffs; have them inscribed inside your contact lenses. Better yet, memorize them. You'll save our Leader a lot of heartache, and you just may put yourself in line for a Cabinet position in some field where you are not an expert but you won't be able to do too much damage. So start memorizing:

ABORTION: A toughie. In Catholic areas you may wish to flatly state, "Abortion is murder," and leave it at that. In most other areas, you can try "What about the rights of the pregnant woman; should she be denied control over her own body, and be forced to carry a prospective child for nine months against her will, and then have to care for him or her for the next eighteen years?"

Always keep in mind, pregnant women can vote; fetuses cannot. Another way to look at it is, a fetus is not fully human until it votes Tory.

AGRICULTURE: We are for it. Say something like "Our Canadian farmers are our most productive citizens: the only disappointing thing about them is that they can vote only once each!" It may get a laugh, and they may even forget to ask you about your agriculture policy, which we are still formulating at the time of this writing.

ARMED FORCES: We need more bangs for not many more seventy-six-cent bucks. (See Chapter Six.)

BAIE COMEAU: A modest shrine will do; a plaque on his birthplace is a must; an airport a possibility.

THE BUDGET: "You'll read about it in the press, just like everyone else. If we talked about it, the Grits would merely steal our ideas, just as they stole Jack Horner — and, with luck, with just as great success." The press will love that one.

BOUEY, GERALD: One more unemployed person in Canada would have no effect upon the statistics. Hell, if Mark McGuigan can joke about firing him, and *he*'s a Grit, then who are we to argue??

CANADAIR: It'll never get off the ground. But where can we find any company stupid enough to buy it? Bailing out Dome was one thing. But Canadair isn't as big or as important. Try something like this: "Let Canada Post handle all Canadair's mailing needs, and Petro Canada pump its gas. That should finish it off."

CAPITAL PUNISHMENT: We think we've found the ideal reply: "It should be a private decision between a murderer and his executioner." By the time they figure *that* one out, you could be in the next province.

CIVIL SERVICE: Too big, too costly, but, most of all, too Liberal. We will have to cut it down to size. But we'll need something a bit more subtle than a straight karate chop.

CROW'S NEST PASS: No matter what you say on this one, they'll have you eating crow. Take a pass. *N'est-ce pas?*

CRUISE MISSILE: We are members of NATO; we have responsibilities to our fellow fighters against the evils of godless Communism. With that said, let me remind you that a majority of Canadians are displeased with the testing of the missile in this country. So try to pull a Joan Rivers; say something like "We feel strongly that the cruise missile should be tested, but that it should be done over an area where there is no intelligent life, such as any locality which has consistently voted Liberal — or even NDP."

DEFICIT: Too big. It will have to be cut, but without raising taxes or harming the universality of social programs. This, of course, is an impossibility, but then so was a Tory majority, just a few short years ago. And politics is the art of the impossible, is it not?

DE HAVILLAND: "To air is human; to lose millions, indefensible."

THE DOLLAR: As long as it's only worth about seventy-six cents, U.S., it will muck up the metric system, where a dollar is *supposed* to be worth a hundred pennies. Say something to the effect that "the Canadian dollar shall remain strong, with the Queen smiling proudly, as long as Canadians have jobs and the Tories are in office. We're working on the job part; but we have to count on *you* to keep us in power. Thank you very much." And then leave the stage very, very quickly.

ETHICS: Ridiculous. Say something like: "You didn't see *us Tories* putting cronies into the senate, doing favours for Liberal bagmen, and juggling slush funds, from 1968 to 1984!" While the audience applauds wildly, mumble under your breath, "Of course not! We weren't in power!"

FIRA: A killer. We need foreign investment, but the bastards tend to gobble up Canada when we allow them in. Why not try this inspired line: "FIRA if necessary, but not necessarily FIRA."

FLOATING DOLLAR: We get a sinking feeling about this one. Say something like: "Why don't we throw Gerald Bouey into the Rideau, and see if *he* floats?"

FREE ENTERPRISE: That's what it's all about. We *are* Tories. We recommend that you pick up a copy of *The Wealth of Nations* by Adam Smith. Whenever you are asked about free enterprise, just pluck a line or two from Smith's masterpiece. They will be so impressed that you read ancient economic texts, you'll gain hundreds of votes right there.

(If any reporter actually knows about the book, which is highly doubtful, and asks whether something two hundred years old can possibly be relevant in the 1980s, just tell him or her to shut up.)

FREE TRADE: Easier said than done. Those damned Japanese didn't *really* lose the war, did they? We would *love* to have free trade, but the Asians and some of the Europeans would eat us *alive*. Why not try this superb line, recently thought up by one of our high paid staff researchers (and a *girl*, yet): "Free trade if possible, but not possibly free trade."

INDIANS: We have no reservations about supporting them in their demands for self-rule. That's a pun, just in case you missed it.

JOBS, JOBS, JOBS: See UNEMPLOYMENT.

LANGUAGE RIGHTS: This depends upon the province and the specific group you are speaking to. When in real doubt, call 996-PARL in Ottawa (area code 613).

LITERACY: We need to make sure that more and more Canadians use more and more four-letter words, such as VOTE and TORY.

LABOUR: They often vote NDP, which is a comment on *their* literacy, but they are still an important facet of our land. Say "We recognize the major role which labour has played in our work force, and we support their right to work anywhere they please." Something like that.

LOBBIES: Love 'em. You'll get free dinners, free gifts for the wife and kids, free advice, and lots and lots of great mailings, which the children can use in class projects. Ignore them at your peril. They often — literally — pay your salary.

MARIJUANA: Thanks to Grit mismanagement, a nickel bag now costs as much as a dime or a quarter. Furthermore, Grenada Gold and San Salvador Silver have become far more difficult to obtain, due to the political machinations of the Reagan government in Central and South America. All in all, it's not worth it. We recommend Scotch on the rocks. It can give you just as good a buzz, just as fast, and it's totally legal.

METRIC: Contrary to certain right-wing opinion (sorry about that, Sinc!), we Tories do *not* consider metrication a Communist plot. We do, however, feel that it has been handled in an arbitrary, mean-spirited, pushy way by the arbitrary, mean-spirited, pushy Grits. Our real fear is that Americans planning a visit to Canada in the summer will phone to ask what the weather is like. On being told "a nice, balmy 25," they will hang up in terror, thinking that the operator meant Fahrenheit.

So, if you are asked about metric, say something like, "If the good Lord, in Her infinite wisdom, wanted us to go metric, She would have given us ten fingers." If this confuses them, remind them of Trudeau's single finger, and go like sixty on to the next topic. (Which is Imperial, we remind you.)

MIDDLE EAST: It stays in Tel Aviv. We don't care if your riding is 99% Jewish. Beyond that, mumble something about being "fair-minded", although that will probably enrage everyone from the Israelis to the PLO. Better just say "Far greater minds than I have said and done idiotic things about the Middle East."

NATO: Piece of cake. This means Not According To Ontario, and refers to when Brian disagrees with Bill Davis about something.

NEGATIVE INCOME TAX: Negative. Hell, why should people get paid for not working? Well, maybe the civil service. But if *everyone* was paid for not working, we'd be in one helluva mess, wouldn't we?

NEP: This was, of course, the National Energy Policy of the Grits, which not only alienated the entire west, and put them firmly into the Tory ranks, but also enraged the States, our greatest, most reliable, and wealthiest ally. For those reasons, we have a two-letter answer to any queries: "PU!"

NUCLEAR POWER: Our opinions have changed radically on this one, especially since Joe Clark was leader, when he once expressed his opinion that the China Syndrome referred to the excessive use of MSG in his chicken-fried rice. As of now, we are *against* the pollution caused by the excessive use of coal; *for* cheap energy; *against* acid rain; *for* the harnessing of hydrogen; and *for* solar power. Make it clear to your constituents that Three Mile Island did *not* occur under a Tory administration, without reminding them that it happened in Pennsylvania.

NUCLEAR WAR: The ultimate downer (see Chapter Six).

OIL PRICES: Try: "We in the great Tory Party believe that the people should pay whatever the traffic will bear. And the traffic has gotten pretty bad recently, hasn't it? It can take an hour to get downtown from the suburbs nowadays, and that's in Hearne, Saskatchewan!" (Foth's home town; he'll love us for that one.) "But a lot depends upon Iran. Ayatollah once, Ayatollah twice, Khomeini times Ayatollah, we've got to dig our own wells, and not depend on others."

OFF-SHORE RIGHTS: Situational answers here, we're afraid. If you are a Newfoundland MP, attack Ottawa. If you represent anywhere else, attack Newfoundland. If you have invested heavily in offshore drilling permits, or in oil firms who have major interests in the area, then just say, "I'll get back to you on that." The line worked remarkably well for Brian for over a year.

PATRONAGE: What's good for Goose Bay is good for Gander. If you are challenged by anyone, ask them if they have ever used the office Xerox to photocopy a recipe for the little woman, or ever taken a towel from a hotel. If they persist, tell them you didn't hear them bitching about the Grits when *they* stole everything but the wallpaper. If they still persist, remind them that this is Canada and not the U.S., and "Let him who is without chin, cast the first stone." (First said by Joe Clark, June 1983, Ottawa Civic Centre.)

PETRO-CANADA: Say this: "The government of Canada has no place in the gas stations of the nation." Or, "Any name which reads so well in both official languages can't be *all* bad. Look at CBC and Radio Canada!" Use the former line in the west; the latter in the east.

POLLS: Tell them, "The only poll that counts is the one taken on election day." If it shows us way ahead, say, "Naturally we are pleased, but the only poll that counts is the one taken on election day." If it shows us way behind, say, "This is obviously the twentieth poll, since they say they are correct nineteen out of twenty times. But the only poll that counts is the one taken on election day." If the poll shows us being creamed and eaten alive, and it was taken by our own pollsters and then leaked by some mole, say, "From Steve Podborski to Peter Gzowski, Poles have helped make this country great."

PORN: The best stuff comes from BC, in both VHS and Beta. Wait for the post-Christmas sales, and have it mailed to a private post-office box. Ontario may crack down soon, even on mail-orders, so get a PO box in Hull and check it out every week.

Now, as to questions from the press, answer: "Violence against women is intolerable. My mother was a woman, my wife is a woman, my daughter is a future woman (if you have a daughter). I would never hit any of them, although God knows they have occasionally given me cause. Pornography which shows violence against women is intolerable. Pornography which shows love for women is quite another matter, however. Pornography which shows love for a number of women at the same time is extremely exciting to some, but offensive to others, and we have to be tolerant of different views. Views through bedroom windows, for instance, can be one kind; views through a keyhole can be another. Voyeurism is what it is called. It's not terribly violent, unless they break down the door." At this point, you'd better move on to the next question. Quickly.

POT: See MARIJUANA. But not too often, and not in public.

QUEBEC: One of the ten great provinces of this blessed land.

Say something like, "Now that Quebec has seen the light, and no longer throws its lot in with the wretched Grits, we feel that Quebec deserves a fair shake! No longer will it be treated as Lower Canada! It will get the upper hand from us! And a firm, solid hand, too!" Say this in French, and be prepared for a standing ovation. When in the west, say this in French and, since they won't understand a word you are saying, you may get a standing ovation there too. You really can't lose if you'll only use your languages carefully, and in the proper places.

RCMP: Our beloved men in red. Here's your chance to give a real barn-burner of a speech. Try this one: "From Nelson Eddy and Jeanette Mac-Donald to the wire-tapping of today, the Royal Canadian Mounted Police have helped settle this country, from Hollywood to the Yukon. In the words of a great Canadian, 'Moderation in defence of liberty is no virtue. Extremism in pursuit of victory is no vice!' ''

REVENUE CANADA: ''No one likes to pay income tax. I know I personally hate to pay income tax. But I do think we all have an obligation to pay our income tax, and preferably before April 30, or we could be fined. As the judge said to the inebriated weatherman, ''Fine today, cooler tomorrow!'' (I love it! — Brian)

RIGHT TO STRIKE: Where would our baseball pitchers be without it?

ROYAL COMMISSIONS: Don't leave home without one, to paraphrase a great commercial. If it weren't for Royal Commissions, we would have to *act* on some of the most painful, controversial, vote-losing topics and problems of our day. Royal Commissions are worth every penny. They are worth every dollar, too!

SEALS: If only they weren't so damned *cute*. Yet they are an important part of the Newfoundland economy, bringing many hundreds of dollars every year into Peckford's coffers. Then again, many countries are boycotting Canadian companies because of our murder of the little critters, leading to the loss of many *millions* of dollars from our Ottawa coffers. Which means we have to stand for something. So let's try:

''We are against the abortion of baby seals. We are against the murder of baby seals, unless the baby seal has killed a police officer in the line of duty. We do not believe that baby seals should partake in the illegal use of drugs. The use of baby seals in kiddie porn films for filthy-minded adult seals is abhorrent to me and, I am sure, to all right-thinking Canadians. In brief, the seal hunt should be called off, unless it can be done in secret and without the knowledge of Greenpeace. Finally, if baby seals *must* be put to death, they should be given extreme unction in both official languages, as well as Newf. When requested. Amen.''

THE SENATE: See PATRONAGE. Also Chapter Three. If you've *really* been good, see Brian.

SIX AND FIVE: Good numbers to play in Lottario, but rather silly anywhere else.

SLUSH FUNDS: An outrage. A Grit tool for staying in power. What can you expect from the socialists?

(If they are accusing Tories of having them: "We know nothing about this.")

SPY BILLS: Pay them before the due date, or get hit with a penalty.

TAXES: See REVENUE CANADA, above. Furthermore, since we stand for tradition and continuity, taxes are something we have to support. Also, if it weren't for taxes, where do you think we'd get the money to pay your salary? Eh?

UNEMPLOYMENT: We prefer "between jobs", although the public tends to get nasty when it's been "between jobs" for more than ten years. Try something like "Unemployment is necessary, but not necessarily unemployment." A great line thought up by one of our highly paid research team.

UNIVERSALITY OF SOCIAL PROGRAMS: We'll get back to you on this one.

WAGE AND PRICE CONTROLS: We don't mind the Wage Controls, but those Price Controls will have to go.

THE WEST: A fabulous part of the country, which we can heartily recommend for vacations. The Rockies are gorgeous. Most important, they've got lots and lots of oil, and there is nary a Liberal in sight. There used to be Socialists in Manitoba, but not since they began to trip over their tongues. (Both official tongues, in fact!) If things ever get too rough in Ottawa, and your constituents start driving you bats, we truly urge you to take a free Air Canada pass for you and your loved ones and check the area out.

WOMEN'S RIGHTS: The hand that cradles the rock, etc. As was mentioned earlier, women *can* vote. They have had the franchise since 1916 in Manitoba; since 1922 in nearly all other provinces; and since 1940 in Quebec. Federally (alas!) they've been able to have their say since 1918. (Is there any truth to the allegation that "Men are right, but women are

NDP?'' Are broads really *that* bent?) However, with education and a growing maturity we continue to hope that the fair sex will begin to use their votes more intelligently and more *conservatively*. Once they get to know Brian better.

In the meantime, they are causing problems. Some of them are even starting to use their own names (a few of you may be less surprised than others on this one). And the things they're demanding! Equal pay! Daycare! And, most troublesome of all, the Right to Control Their Own Bodies — when, in the good old days, we men did a perfectly acceptable job of controlling their bodies for them!

But we must face facts: they are in the majority now, and don't you forget it. They carry a lot of clout and cannot be ignored. (Especially when they raise their voices.) After all, if your riding was 54% Inuit, would you ignore their demands?

If your riding was 54% Catholic, would you march in the Orange Day Parade?

If your riding was 54% Jewish, would you fight to move the Canadian Embassy to Jerusalem? *You bet you wouldn't.*

Anyway, the girls outnumber us now, thanks to our male eating (and drinking) habits, overwork, and confusion of sexual roles. So we cannot ignore their demands. Still, they are not all without humour, except for the real libbers, who aren't in a majority yet. So the next time you are questioned about Daycare, Equal Pay, or The Right To Control, etc., just answer, slowly and deliberately, raising your hand to your head in mock pain, ''Oh! I'm sorry! But I've got a headache!'' (For more on this admittedly tedious subject, see Chapter Eight.)

What to Cry Out in Parliament

Not everything in Parliament is as terrifying as Question Period (see ''Witty Repartee'', below.) Not by a long shot. Indeed, often you will see and hear one of your own beloved Cabinet Ministers speak on a major topic of the day, risking the Liberals stealing all our great ideas.

A Glossary of Question-Period Gestures

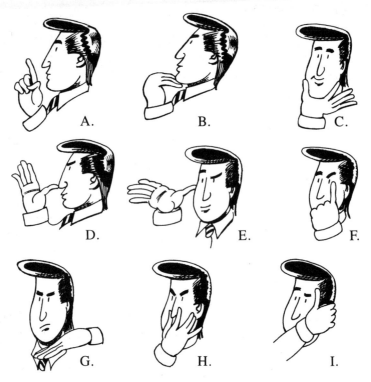

A. "The Honourable Member need not speak when he has nothing to say."

B. "Mr. Speaker, in these tough times, we say to the Opposition, 'Chins up.'"

C. Thinking.

D. "I salute the Honourable Member's opinion."

E. "The Honourable Member's private bill, Mr. Speaker, is as feasible as a flying penguin."

F. "We acknowledge we're looking at the best Opposition money can buy. Shows how far the currency has fallen."

G. "As it has been said before, we won't dignify that question with a yes or no answer."

H. "That question is typical of the usual level attained by the Opposition."

I. "Question period is almost over. Tell Mila to put on the coffee."

Anyway, when your beloved Cabinet Minister speaks you must listen attentively, and be prepared to cry out.

1. Whenever in doubt, yell, "HEAR! HEAR!"

2. Whenever *really* in doubt, yell, "WHERE? WHERE?"

3. Whenever the Right Honourable Joseph Clark speaks, yell, "WHO? WHO?"

4. Whenever someone in the Tory ranks says something funny, yell, "HA! HA!"

Practise these until you get them exactly right. Your constituents at home, your Cabinet Ministers, and, most important, Brian will be pleased that you did.

Witty Repartee in the House of Commons

As we have noted elsewhere, Question Period is now televised, so the chances of you guys impressing the hell out of your constituents are phenomenal. Not all of us are naturally witty and funny, like Brian, so we are here making a series of suggestions (with the occasional warning, in parentheses), of what to shout during a particularly sharp debate or argument in the House.

Use these sparingly, but for God's sake *use* them. And if you can think of any which are wittier or more to the point, please call 996-QUIP in Ottawa (area code 613), and share them with your fellow Tories.

Remember, the following were not just tossed off by some first-time back-bencher from northern Labrador! These have been worked over, and refined, by some of the best comedy writers in Los Angeles (since we couldn't find any good ones in Canada). Go to it, Tories!

NYAA NYAA, DEE NYAA NYAA!!

SIT DOWN!!

OH, YEAH!?? WELL, I BET YOUR MOTHER WEARS BASIC TRAINING WHEELS ON HER ARMY BOOTS!!

DOWN IN FRONT!!

IF YOU HAD ONE BRAIN CELL, IT WOULD DIE OF LONELINESS!!

YEAH? YOU'RE LIKE YOUR DAD. *HE* COULDN'T LICK A POSTAGE STAMP, EITHER!!

MY HONOURABLE FRIEND, YOU COULDN'T ORGA-NIZE A PISS-UP IN A BREWERY!!

FAGGOT!

AS FOR THE HONOURABLE HOSE-HEAD OPPO-SITE. . . .

ORDER!! ORDER!!

ODOUR!! ODOUR!!

YOU'RE A GREAT EXAMPLE OF WHY DONKEYS NEVER GO TO COLLEGE — NO ONE LIKES A SMART ASS!!

YOU WEAR LOAFERS 'CAUSE YOU'RE TOO DUMB TO TIE YOUR OWN SHOES!

SISSY!!

WHY DON'T YOU GO BACK WHERE YOU CAME FROM?

YOU SHOULDN'T HAVE RUN FOR OFFICE — YOU SHOULD'VE RUN FOR COVER!!

I APOLOGIZE TO THE HONOURABLE MEMBER OPPOSITE. AS A GRIT, I DIDN'T REALIZE HE'D STOOP SO HIGH!

SHUT UP!!

NINCOMPOOP!

YOU'RE A GREAT ARGUMENT FOR HIRING THE MENTALLY INCOMPETENT!

CROOK!

YOUR MOTHER SHOULD HAVE BELIEVED IN ABORTION!

WHICH OFFICIAL LANGUAGE WAS *THAT* STUTTERED IN??

THAT'S THE BEST EUGENE WHELAN IMITATION I'VE EVER HEARD!

BRING BACK TRUDEAU!

How to Handle the NDP

Newer members of Parliament, who just joined us in Ottawa with our latest sweep into Power, may not be familiar with the NDP.

The New Democratic Party is a purportedly national political party of the socialist bent, not unlike the national Liberal Party, which has done barely better, in terms of votes and numbers of Members of Parliament. The NDP grew out of the CCF, which stood for Cancel Canada's Freedoms, which pretty well tells it all, doesn't it?

To be fair, the NDP *did* help run Canada (into the ground) back in

1972-74, when the Liberals had a minority government and needed their numbers.

With the coming to power of the Progressive Conservatives in 1984, under the inspired leadership of Brian Mulroney, the NDP found itself between a Chin and a Squishy Place, and was destined to irrelevancy and political doom.

Which brings us back to the title of this section (see above). For the answer, a brief analogy:

What do you do when you are driving sixty miles an hour (oops! — a hundred kilometres an hour), and some flies and bugs get squashed all over your windshield? Why, you just stop, get out of your car, and flick them off the glass.

Same with the NDP.

CHAPTER FIVE

The — Uh! — Dollar, and How to Spend It

The Tory View on Economics

Come on. You know what economics is. Or should that be what economics *are*? It's really quite simple, just like all the answers to unemployment, defence, the deficit: you incur debts in the guise of monthly bills. You borrow money to improve your lodgings, your lifestyle, your credit rating. You labour to obtain the liquid capital to amortize your debts. The idea is to bring in sufficient or more monies than you put out.

And that's it! Basic economics! Balancing your bank book! Ends meeting! It *sounds* simple enough: good, plain, conservative fiscal management.

So why isn't this fundamental accountability and control—the new Motherhood issue — applied to government?

Why not, indeed? Because this is the Big League! This is balancing the *banks'* books. This is standing on the corner of Dun and Bradstreet with your dancing monkey. This is the world of deficit financing. Now, if you *still* cannot see what's involved here, we recommend that you observe the situation by standing on your head.

To begin with, which is a perfect place to start, you must memorize the following statement about governmental economics: ''The observation of realities has never, to put it mildly, been one of the strengths of economic development theory.'' That was spoken by Jane Jacobs, who is a woman. She is also originally from the States, which may impress you more. In simpler words, for any of you who have only recently had the sense to join our Party, economics is the unbridled ability to spend money for no one's general amusement.

And so we come to contract, or civil service, economists (with an accent on the last syllable) (*Mists* — get it?). These are ersatz sages and oracles who have had the temerity to deem that poking around in chicken entrails, inducing visions by chemical means, and sticking a licked finger heavenwards to determine economic wind direction, should be recognized as profound wisdom, worthy of professional rates.

And that is a kindly comment, in terms of estimating their actual worth. So, apart from placing a lien on the Alberta Heritage Fund, or convincing Wayne Gretzky to become the Bank of Canada (at least during off-season), we must have, if not *concrete* economic solutions, then at least the basic terminology to *buy us time*.

And that is where you come in. You must become well versed in the theories propounded by the major economists.

For instance, what is meant by the demand-side theory of economic expansion?

Concisely, it means that the demand for goods and services leads the way in an expanding, prosperous economy. Or Keynesianism, if you wish. (Which, as Tories, we would normally *not* wish. But these are not normal times in which we live.)

And what do we mean by supply-side economics?

Adam Smith can take the blame for this theory. He attributed economic expansion to expanding production and trade. *Et voilà!* The inspiration for Reaganism and Thatcherism, economically speaking. (But Smith cannot be held accountable for Lebanon and the Falklands.)

Okay. So now we have supply-side economics and demand-side economics. And, defying all the laws of mechanics and gravity (see Galileo and Newton on those), we have, like ants at a picnic, stagflation.

Yep: high unemployment coupled with rising prices. This has become known as sui-cide economics.

So what is our plan?

Call it blind-side economics. In brief, this is how it will work:

Basically, the strategy is to attack the problems from unexpected angles. And the penalty goes to the *victim*, not the attacker! Smart, eh?

We Tories feel that we must start over, unfettered by the Gritty past, on to the Road to Recovery. Which means novel points of departure.

For example, we *could* start a war (not nuclear, of course, just a *small* war!) and depend on the kindness of strangers (read victors, not Blanche DuBois) for the rebuilding of our country, like an updated version of the Marshall Plan. In the grand tradition of *The Mouse That Roared*, this is referred to as macro-economics.

When the fiscal assistance Peter-principle's out, and we petition for more aid, we are in a state dubbed by the donor "holy macro-economics!"

Unfortunately, the circumstance of our war readiness (to use the phrase extremely loosely; see Chapter Six) denies us much opportunity (read: no opportunity) to ease our chronic unemployment through the setting up of munitions factories.

A better contrivance: abolish savings. Eliminate dollar-*angst*. The dollar would be revalued as worthless, in line with the value already opined by world money merchants.

Think of it! There are many wonderful aftermaths of this inspired stratagem, for which we thank John Crosbie, the former finance critic:

Rising costs: With no money, how can you have rising costs?

Inflation: Multiply anything by zero, and what do you get? We could have the inflation rate of Israel, multiplied by the inflation rate of Argentina, and still be able to legitimately treat it as nothing.

National debt: We declare bankruptcy. It worked for Dome; it worked for Chrysler; it worked for Cleveland. We've got nothing to lose and our creditors would have *lots* of nothing to gain. Although we wouldn't bank on it, if we were them. Which we *are*, to a point.

Government spending: For years, the public have complained that the government does nothing for them. Now we will be able to spend accordingly.

Taxation reform: Automatic! Revenue Canada would begin to mail out T-zero forms. This form would simply notify the department that the public was, indeed, not accumulating the former coin of the realm, unless of course they were doing it for antiquarian or hobbyist purposes, for which permission would be granted automatically.

Civil servants in this department would be shifted to Confidential Canada. To dismiss them outright would constitute a gross waste of valuable training and skills, which would require no substantial upgrading in department transference, and at great non-cost to the public lack-of-purse.

Transfer of payments to provinces: What payments?

Pensions: All Canadians will go to their great reward. But not *all* of us can be appointed to the Senate, especially those who have consistently voted Grit, PQ, NDP, Rhinoceros, or anything to do with Paul Hellyer.

So what is the great reward, you ask? We are negotiating with Grenada, St. Vincent, and the Grenadines (which is *not* the famed Jesuit singing group, by the way), St. Lucia, Martinique, Dominica, Guadeloupe, Antigua, Barbados, Montserrat, Nevis, Basseterre, Anguilla, and British Columbia, to become Official Canadian Retirement Habitats. Provincial status would be proffered to each of the aforementioned Caribbean Islands, as each qualifies admirably with our proposed new monetary system. Namely, they are worth nothing as well.

Medicare: This perennial dilemma would also be solved through our new concept for economic reform. After all, how can one put a value on medical services? You can't — so why bother? And if doctors, nurses, and other practitioners of the art of healing have no money problems, they can get on with what they do best.

The economy: How will it function without money? Why, the same way it does now. Only we Tories propose to raise the prosperous economy above ground, to propriety.

What are we talking about? The barter system. You see, in the past, billions in goods and services exchanged hands without the divine intervention of Revenue Canada. In the old system, Revenue Canada got nothing from these millions of transactions, and that status quo will be maintained, thus perpetuating the admirable trait of continuance of tradition so central to Tory thought. Our motto, as always: "Go from it to a new future" — the polls willing.

Unemployment: This is, we admit, a hard nut to crack. We *could* strike unemployment from the canon of economic woe by merely reclassifying it as Neo-Luddites, or Third-Wave-Leisurites, or Indigentellectuals, or, most conveniently, British Columbians.

As the unemployed are actually workers who are not compensated for their unapplied services, they could now be thought of as Workers Who Have Been In The Vanguard Of The New Anti-Monetarism.

Before we Tories came to power, it used to be said, "Give 'em a dollar's dollar. The public deserves its two cents' worth." Now they won't even get that. But then again, neither will anyone else.

We hope we have made ourselves perfectly clear. Any questions? Just call our toll-free number, 995-DIME (area code 613), from any riding in Canada outside Ottawa. In the capital, give us a dingle at 996-COIN.

Recommendations for Lowering the Budget Deficit

The Liberals have really blown it, this time—and we mean blown it *up*! The deficit in the Federal Budget is horrendous, and we just *have* to get it down. Not *too* quickly, mind you; we've got to beef up the Armed Forces, hand out a lot of plush jobs, expensive patronage, etc. Still, it really *has* to come down, or we are going to find ourselves in Big Trouble. Now, no one says we will be able to get it down as successfully as Ronnie, down in the States. But most of us feel it *has* to be cut down, well below $20 billion, by the time our first five-year term of office is complete. Okay, maybe $25 billion — but not a penny more.

Look, we just *may* be willing to let it hover around $30 billion, but certainly no higher.

Certainly, if we can keep it under $45 billion, that will be a *far* lower increase than took place under the free-spending Grits, wouldn't it?

Anyway, some well-thought-out ideas on "How to Lower the Budget Deficit", from many months of economic tinkering and doodling:

1) Borrow from Peter Lougheed at Favourable Rates of Interest: This is also known in the caucus as "Privatizing the Heritage Fund". It might well cause tensions between Alberta and Ottawa, but when we consider the feelings between that province and our country's capital under the Grits, it couldn't possibly be worse.

2) Merge de Havilland and Canadair: Many of you may wonder about the thought behind this kind of merger. Then again, many of you may wonder why our country has been throwing bad money after bad for the last few decades, under the spendthrifts who preceded us to office.

    But our reasoning is simple. So simple, in fact, it's rather surprising the idiot Grits didn't think of it first: Every grade-school math student knows that two negatives make a positive! So if we merge two such losers as de Havilland

and Canadair, just maybe they'll turn around in this classic mathematical fashion.

3) Take Many Unemployed Tories Off the Streets and Place Them in Government Jobs, Where They Will Pay Taxes Instead of Collecting Unemployment Insurance and Welfare: Self-evident.

4) Kill Universality of Certain Government Programs, Such as Giving Monthly Baby Bonuses to Millionaires: Sorry, fellas. There are some cows which are simply too sacred to touch, and the universality of baby bonuses is one of them. Remember the slurs in England about "Thatcher the Milk Snatcher" because she voted down federal funds for kids' milk? Do we want to end up like her?
On second thought. . . .

Brother, Can You Spare a Buck: The Canadian Dollar

Under the Grits, need we remind you, the Canadian dollar shrank so much it couldn't cover a flea's navel, much less the total bill of a subsidized meal in the parliamentary cafeteria.

If Grit fiscal policy is perpetuated any longer, the dollar will soon be equal to the Romanian shekel.

Our policy is that this incredible shrinkage *must be arrested*—if necessary, by the RCMP—or else Romania will be buying our CANDU reactors for $2,099 each.

The answer is simple. So simple, in fact, we got the idea from our neighbourhood dry-cleaning establishment: We Tories propose to Sanforize the buck. Either that, or make it out of polyester. (Ever throw a pair of cotton pants into the washer with a pair of polyester ones? Notice which ones do *not* shrink?)

Failing this, we shall urge upon the Canadian public that we bring back the Diefenbuck. Even at its worst levels, it was still fifteen cents worthier than the True Dough.

Other suggestions, from Mr. Crosbie — for which we thank him greatly: that we rename our dollar "the yen"; it may sound funny, but apparently the term commands great respect on world markets.

Or (thanks again, John) we could print the Canadian dollar the same size as the Italian lira. That way, at least it would *look* big.

CHAPTER SIX

Our Armed Forces — What There is of Them

An Addendum on Our Armed Forces: A Note From Joe Clark

This is a hot flash, so to speak.

A lot of us want to see Canada rearmed, but we are concerned about the expense.

So here's my plan: We can, and should, rearm our beloved country at a fraction of the cost we feared!

Here's how: We should buy state-of-the-art weaponry, but it should be state-of-the-art *circa* 1980 or 1981. We would buy it from private arms merchants. The experience alone would do wonders for multiculturalism; imagine our soldiers trying to read the directions on the Russian, Israeli, and Brazilian warranties!

It's like buying a used car, or a 1984 just when the 1985 models come out — it's still top quality, but it's a year (or two, or three or four) old. Who cares if it won't get as much at trade-in time? Who on earth trades in an Exocet missile, or an Uzi machine-gun?

Furthermore, why should Canadians — or even our Armed

Forces — be concerned if our weapons are a few years old? We'll never use them anyway! And you have to admit: A four-year-old submarine or a three-year-old rocket-launcher which will just sit, rust, or gather dust/algae is a heck of a lot cheaper, while sitting, than one which just rolled off the assembly lines of Detroit or Leningrad!

The only problem may be that we'll have to compete with the Bolivians at the international arms bazaars, but this could lead to a strong influx of Spanish-speaking civil servants, a welcome addition to our community of communities.

As you can see, we could save many millions of dollars; perhaps even billions. And the general public need never know that we are cutting corners in this manner! They have a sense that their Armed Forces are incapable of saving them from attack, whether from the States or from the USSR, and they are probably correct in that assumption. So if we are going to surrender anyway, then let's do it with far less costly weaponry!

Yours for lower budgets and greater savings,

Respectfully submitted,

The Rt. Hon. Joseph P. Clark

Note from B.M. — I'll take it under advisement, Joe. Thanks for your thoughts. It's clear that you will be a great asset to my administration, or at least part of an asset, if you know what I mean. My regards to Ms. McTeer.

The Canadian Armed Forces: Where's the Beef-Up?

A few years ago, a comedy troupe joked that all Canada needed for its Armed Forces budget was a dime. When we were invaded, the Prime Minister would grab it, drop it into a pay-phone, and call the Russians, crying "We surrender!"

Of course this is no longer true. Today, we would have to provide the PM with a quarter. But the lack of preparedness is worse than ever, and we have good cause for alarm.

Which is why we here present, in black and white — *but for Tory MPs' eyes only* — our Progressive Conservative policy to reinstill pride, reverence, and, most important, lots of big bucks, into our armed services.

1) We should return to the distinctive uniforms for the three services. (Yes, there were once three services; just how old do you have to be to be elected MP, anyway?) It is not our intention to have our military outfitted like washroom attendants on an Austrian passenger train, no matter what the Grits may have preferred. We are going to banish the "Oh, what the Hellyer . . ." attitude which has grown tragically prevalent, and restore a proper *esprit du corpse* (we *know* that isn't the usual spelling!).

2) We need to get some military-minded bureaucrats into the upper echelons of the civil service; people who know the military and its hardware. We do *not* need the types who can't find the men's room without an Armed Forces navigator.

3) We must get our Armed Forces into a better state of combat readiness. We recommend full-scale wargames be carried out at brass-knuckle hamlets, such as Whitney Pier, Nova Scotia, and Prince Rupert, British Columbia.

   If our fighting men and women can survive battles with steelworkers and lumberjacks, and others of similar ilk, we're ready for anything the rest of the world can ever dish out.

4) Arctic sovereignty is most vital. We plan to commission the construction of 5 (five) armed ice-breakers to ply the Arctic seas and maintain one dominion over our Arctic territory.

We will demand that all inhabitants, interlopers, and non-Inuit show diplomatic passports. We intend to establish who's who, even to the extent of arresting aliens — and we don't mean ET, either. A prerequisite for service in this icicle-corps will be a facility with the languages of Russian and American. Our flag will be shown in three languages, with consecutive translation into each.

5) We must increase our participation in NATO. Our efforts to date have placed us in the unenviable state of being considered two steps below the level of POW.

We will issue real rifles, *not* wooden parade dummies as in the past under the Grits. Our Armed Forces radio will carry military information and *not* just the Tommy Hunter transcription series and the 1954 Grey Cup re-broadcasts.

We will supply some Piper Cubs for our air corps, rather than continue to have them jump on trampolines near the contentious border areas.

We will resurrect our single Bomarc missile and fit it out with an *American* nuclear warhead, equivalent to many hundreds of pounds of TNT.

We will paste a photo of Ronald Reagan on its tip.

And finally, to comply with the Americans' desire that we beef up our Armed Forces in Europe, we will open a Wendy's on our base camp at Lahr, Germany. (West Germany, at least so far. But who knows?)

6) We must have our Armed Forces at the ready for civilian policing in domestic trouble zones. These could well include such contentious situations as when the Nordiques play the Canadiens, the Oilers play the Flames, etc. We should thank the Lord God in Heaven that the Expos and the Blue Jays are in separate leagues; it was terrifying enough when Sun Life pulled out of Montreal and moved to Toronto, but a Blue Jay ball club victorious over the

Expos could play right into the slippery hands of Monsieur Lévesque.

All soldiers, including Anglos, *must* be fluent in French. This would become most advantageous when the troops were deployed into such vexacious, contra-linguistic areas as, say, Winnipeg, should the shoving of French down people's throats become federal law and then be disobeyed or resisted.

7) We will fight them in the Arctic, we will fight them on the Prairies, we will fight them in the cities, we will fight them if it takes all night. The Grits have weakened our country far too much; the time to make amends is now. For God and country.

The Canadian Navy, of Blessed Memory

Let's face it. Thanks to our budgetary situation, we can't afford more than one leaky battleship on each coast, each of which takes in more water than it ploughs through.

Indeed, it has been said that the Canadian Navy (to use a phrase loosely) has the only battleships which double as a submarine corps. Some say that makes our forces unique. Others say it makes our forces eunuch. It's all in the way you say it and spell it.

Last spring a cannon on one of our ships went off, and the recoil sent the thing all the way to Moose Jaw. This has to stop. (For one thing, they'll have to ban smoking on deck.)

Some ideas for you to ponder. (Better yet, just to add to your standard speeches.) We need to convince the Inuit hunters in the far north to spear Russian subs in addition to whales. In this way, we'd get some visible minorities into our Armed Forces, and make the Inuit our Northern Defence Line.

Another new concept: In order to keep our costs down on both coasts (and our coasts down at all costs) we should encourage fog, as a bicoastal defence. (For this concept we must thank brother Bill Davis, who has been doing the same in his speeches for years.)

Why fog, you ask? As a great soldier once said — we think it was George Chuvalo — "What ya can't see, ya can't hit." We rest our case.

Peace or War?

A Special Essay by MP from Y-P

There has been a lot of talk about Peace recently, and the fact that it has been the Liberals who have been doing most of the talking should be a matter of concern and wariness for all right-thinking Tories. When Trudeau was Prime Minister for the past few hundred years, he kept screaming Peace, and even hopped all over the globe talking to commies, leftists, pinkos, fellow-travellers, reds, marxists and other bedfellows, all about Peace.

He got good press, but anyone with any brains could see the cynicism behind his moves. Who *isn't* for Peace, for God's sake? It's like coming out for Motherhood! Or Maple Syrup! Or Brian, for that matter.

Anyway, here is my suggestion. (And it is *only* a suggestion, mind you; it should be discussed and voted upon at Tory gatherings, right across Canada, before it becomes our policy.) Why don't we Progressive Conservatives come out for War? (As we already said, *non*-nuclear.) *Think* about it!

It has worked fabulously for Lebanon, for instance. And look at Northern Ireland! Iran! Iraq! Most of the countries in Africa! Even in Argentina, we saw how the Falkland Islands war helped keep the public's worries over runaway inflation and vanished children off their troubled minds.

Now, think of what War would do for Canada! It would certainly help improve our depressed industries (recall, if you will, how World War II snapped Canada out of the Great Depression). The Canadian public would be so wrapped up with any War we declared that all the bitching about inflation, sexism, daycare, abortion, would stop *but quick*. Consider the Tories coming out for war — and think how fast the Grits would try and steal *that* idea from us! Think about it. Why not take over St. Pierre, for a start?

Nuclear War

A definitive word on this subject is essential. All of us realize it could end everything we hold dear: Air Canada passes; slush funds; the Senate. It will also kill just about everybody except the top brass (us). And even *we* won't have much fun when we climb out of our super-shelters.

So, if there has ever been a motherhood issue, this is it. No matter who is in your audience, no matter how economically depressed your riding is, you can count on its being a winner. Rail against it! Perhaps along the following lines:

''Nuclear war is the ultimate obscenity. The definitive holocaust. The war to end all wars (and everything else)! It will make acid rain seem like a pleasant sun-shower. It will wreak havoc with our superb telephone and telecommunications industry. It will create pot-holes in our nation's roads which could prove beyond repair! It will put undue stress upon our medical resources! It will louse up our tourist season completely!'' (Get really riled up now.) ''Nuclear war is *unthinkable*! I don't even *want* to think about it! And I don't want *you* to think about it either! So let's not have another word about nuclear war, eh?''

Only a nut would be *for* nuclear war, and most of them are down in the States, making big bucks and voting Republican. We can afford to lose their votes, so stand up tall on this one — you really can't lose.

New Armed Forces Uniform
A welcome return to Canadian tradition. The thin red line and all that. *"Maintiens le droit."*

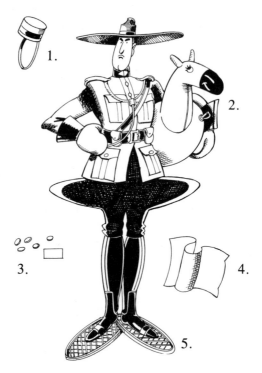

1. Pillbox Mountie hat. For entertaining visiting U.S. military VIPs. Yanks like bellhops.

2. Inflatable marine vehicle. Release air from inflation nozzle to facilitate high speed, albeit short, chases.

3. Quarters and a card bearing Pentagon scramble telephone number.

4. In case of nuclear attack, a white flag. Wave frantically at incoming missiles, then attempt to crawl under it. (The flag, not the missile.)

5. Northern transportation.

CHAPTER SEVEN

The (Pardon Us!) Ethnic Question

Pivnicki Ends in "i" and Other Ways of Courting the Ethnic Vote

As you more than likely know by now, Brian Mulroney is of Irish background. And his lovely, vivacious, and stay-at-home wife is the daughter of immigrants of Yugoslavian background. The family name is Pivnicki, and although we are relieved that she changed it, as all women, however modern, should, we must still play on it as much as possible. This is no WASP maiden here, gang: this is a real, live, voting ETHNIC, and we Tories haven't had very many of them over the years.

Until *now*. So the question is, how do we use the Pivnicki name and background to attract ethnic votes?

It's simple. And here is the answer, in black and white (whose votes are also welcome, by the way): use Yugoslavian recipes whenever possible, at fund-raisers.

Now, you may argue, "But the Yugoslavian vote is limited in my riding!"

So you think. But just add Yugoslavian touches to every traditional ethnic dish, and you'll get them coming and going!

Some examples:

> Chicken soup at a Jewish fund-raising dinner? Add spicy borscht, and think Slav.

> Spaghetti at an Italian church banquet? Toss in a few frozen perogies.

> Perogies at a Ukrainian bash? Serve them on plates with drawings of Tito on them.

> Dim sum at a Chinese brunch? See frozen perogies, above.

> Huge Greek salad at a Mediterranean gathering? Just sprinkle in some hot red peppers.

> Paella at a Spanish or Portuguese do? Throw in anything Yugoslavian. Paella is really a garbage-can of food anyway, and they won't suspect a *thing*. (Nor will they taste it, either. But in their subconscious they'll be thinking Yugoslavian, and that's what we're after.)

That's enough. We're getting hungry just thinking about it.

Remember this one thing, most of all: There is absolutely *no* reason, no *logical, thoughtful, intelligent* reason, why anyone should vote for us just because our Beloved Leader happens to have a beautiful, attractive, traditional wife who just happened to come from a country which suffered great Communist repression.

But so what? If politics were logical, people would have been voting in Tory majorities *years* ago. And if reminding the unwashed masses that Brian had the good sense to change an ethnic name to *his*, then use it to the hilt.

Happy eating. And *think Slav*. Better yet, as the Great Weird Al once said, *eat* it! And *he*'s ethnic, too!

Some Mila Dishes

No matter what you serve at your church lunches and fund-raising dinners, the name of the dish is crucial—which is why we are including the following list of recommended dishes, which will remind your constituents of the boss's wife's background.

LASAGNE PIVNICKI

EGG FOO PIVNICKI

SURF & TURF PIVNICKI (to be served at Newfie gatherings)

SUSHNICKI (To be frank, this is Serbo-Croatian food that you forgot to cook; serve *al dente*)

EGGS PIVNICKI (Use Bel Grade-A products, only)

TITO-BURGERS (made with hamburger meat which has been frozen four or more years)

VITAMINS: A & D, E, and a-Serbic acid, all washed down with TORY-BLUE-RIBBON BEER

Happy Eating! (*Bon appetit!*)

French Phrases You Should Know

by John Crosbie

There is a story told, fellow Tories, about a mother mouse and her baby who were suddenly cornered by a giant cat. As the baby mouse whimpered in terror, the mother mouse suddenly cried out, "Growl! Ruff! Ruff!"

The cat spun about and raced out of the house, whereupon the mother looked down at her young and declared, "As I've always said, there's much to be gained from knowing a second language!"

How true. Some of you may be familiar with the problems which *I* have faced, due to my own lack of a second language. (Actually a third language, since I *do* speak Newfoundland.) Well, I have been studying, as I promised at the time I ran against our present beloved leader, and I have been asked to share some of my insights into the beauties of *français* with all of you. Whether you are an MP from Quebec, or from the most Ukrainian area of Saskatchewan, a knowledge of both our official languages is simply a *must*. Try out some of the following words and phrases, noting their meaning well. And all the best o' luck, me boy!

A barbe de fol, on apprend à raire: If you supported Joe Clark, all the more reason that you should support Brian Mulroney.

A beau jeu, beau retour: You vote for me, I'll get you big federal projects in your riding.

Allons, enfants de la patrie! Get your 5-year-olds to vote Tory.

Après moi le déluge: Stick with the Tories, or Trudeau may try to make a comeback.

La belle dame sans merci: Maureen McTeer has as much right to speak as any other Tory.

Le bon Dieu est toujours du côté des gros bataillons: Rebuild the Canadian Armed Forces before it's too late.

Cherchez la femme: What to do during boring Tory weekend caucuses.

Le coeur a ses raisons que la raison ne connaît pas: Vote Tory.

Dans le doute, abstiens-toi: The Canadian Embassy looks just fine in Tel Aviv, doesn't it?

Le demi-monde: Hull, Quebec.

Du sublime au ridicule il n'y a qu'un pas: Do you want Brian Mulroney, or Joe Clark?

Faux pas: Voting Liberal or NDP.

Les femmes peuvent tout parce qu'elles gouvernent les personnes qui gouvernent tout: Equal pay for equal work should be considered.

Il est bon de parler, et meilleur de se taire: The Liberals steal all our best ideas, so shut up.

Il n'y a que ceux qui ne font rien, qui ne se trompent pas: Tel Aviv is a great place to have an embassy.

Il n'y a rien de mieux à faire que de s'amuser: Question period.

Je ne sais quoi: The all-purpose right answer to everything.

Maison de santé: The Parliament Buildings.

Mais où sont les neiges d'antan?: Vacation in Florida for the *Québecois* vote.

Le monde va de lui-même: The Civil Service.

L'occasion fait le larron: The Senate has many openings.

Parole d'honneur: Absolutely nothing.

La patience est amère, mais son fruit est doux: Gays usually vote Grit.

Les plus sages ne le sont pas toujours: Brian knows best.

Prenez garde! Always count heads before the Budget is read.

Le roi le veut: Brian knows best.

Tout est bien qui finit bien: Vote Conservative.

Vers libre: Words are cheap.

Vive la bagatelle! May the Tories be in power for a generation!

I hope the above mini-dictionary of key French phrases will help you to gain and retain power, wherever you may be.

J.C.

German Phrases You May Wish to Know

by John Crosbie

You could all learn a good lesson from my big mistake in the Progressive Conservative leadership campaign of last summer. (The other mistake was running at all against our superb leader, the Right Honourable Brian Mulroney.)

Perhaps you remember: I lost my cool, when questioned by reporters in Longueuil, Quebec, back on May 26, 1983. The dirty mainlanders kept pressing me on my lack of knowledge of French, and I finally exploded, "I cannot talk to the Chinese people in their own language either. . . . I cannot talk to the German people in their own language. Does that mean that there should be no relationship between Canada and China, or Canada and Germany, or whatever?"

Well, a lot of historians believe that I threw it all away that day by comparing knowledge of French — which, after all, *is* one of our two official languages, something I hadn't realized before that day — and such relatively obscure tongues as Chinese and German.

But they are *not* obscure! And there are many perfectly good voters out there, across our wide and glorious land, who *do* speak Chinese and German! So why not learn to talk to them in *their* languages, just as I am so astutely learning French, at the very moment I dictate this?

Now, Chinese is extremely difficult, I confess. But how about Germany, now one of our great allies in Europe, and — far more important — a country which has given us tens of thousands of its people, as immigrants, POWs, etc?

So, for those of you MPs who may have German-speaking people in your riding, here are some good phrases to know:

Adel sitzt im Gemüte nicht im Geblüte: Brian's a great guy.

Die alten zum rat, die jungen zur tat: Stanfield was fine, but Mulroney is really on the ball.

Borgen macht Sorgen: We've *got* to get the federal deficit down!

Danke schön: Vote for me, and I'll build a $200 million domed stadium in your riding.

Deutschland, Deutschland über alles: No one will be extradited from Canada without a fair trial.

Eine Schwalbe macht keinen Sommer: Sure we made mistakes under Joe Clark, but give us a chance *this* time.

Es wird nichts so schön gemacht/Es kommt einer der's veracht': The caucus is totally behind Brian Mulroney.

Eine feste Burg ist unser Gott: Brian can't lose.

Das fünfte Rad am Wagen: We will find an important post for Joe Clark.

Ein gebranntes Kind scheut das Feuer: We do not plan to move the Canadian Embassy in Israel *anywhere*.

Gott macht gesund, und der Doktor bekommt das Geld: The Tories are firmly against extra billing.

Küche, Kirche und Kinder: The Tories care about the feelings of women.

Morgen, morgen, nur nicht heute, sagen alle faule Leute: We hope to act on the question as soon as possible.

Neue Besen kehren gut: Civil servants have nothing to worry about, if they are competent and good workers.

Die Religion ist das Opium des Volkes: I am honoured to be speaking in your church today.

Was ich nicht weiss, macht mich nicht heiss: I shall be calm about the problems we all face.

Wie gewonnen, so zerronnen: If Brian should choose to step down, I would be proud to step into his shoes.

I hope this little German lesson will be of some assistance in your search for their vote.

J.C.

Multiculturalism

Easy. Just repeat the following sentence about two dozen times, and it will be yours for ever: "This great land of Canada has been made even greater through the arrival of millions of people from across this great globe. People from everywhere! England! Europe! Asia! Africa! South America! The Caribbean! Newfoundland! Many have been visible minorities, many invisible, but all indivisible." (Note from Brian: I *love* that last line. Who wrote it? That could guarantee a Senate seat.) "And there is no reason whatsoever why all of these individuals should not practise the religions they want, believe in the things they believe in no matter how odd, and speak the languages they grew up speaking no matter how peculiar they sound. Nor, for that matter, is there any reason whatsoever why we should *pay* for those people to practise their religions and speak their languages! We're trying to cut the deficit, you know! Do your own thing on your own time, and with your own expense account, thank you!"

NB: The last three sentences of the set speech, above, are slightly controversial, and should only be used in Anglo-Saxon ridings. Where there are more than, say, 15% of any minority group which has an odd religion and a peculiar language, better drop it and end with "No matter how peculiar they may sound." And throw in the "Thank you." They seem to love politeness out there, nowadays. It's all part of the Conservative backlash which swept us back into power.

Bilingualism

A no-win. As of the fall of 1984, when this went to press, we are for bilingualism in Manitoba, hoping for bilingualism in Ontario, and feel that the English should have a chance to speak their language in Quebec. But each of these could change, up to 180 degrees, with each passing day. Say something like "THIS COUNTRY WAS FOUNDED BY TWO NATIONS," and hope that they'll let it go at that.

And please — try to learn French; look what it did for Brian!*

---

* Note to John Crosbie: Please try to learn English

CHAPTER EIGHT

Other—Possibly Vital— Matters

Women in Politics: or Brian's Pro-Menstrual Syndrome

Let us be frank—this *is* a thorny issue. One cannot afford to sound too glib or puckish. One must remain objective. We therefore offer you the following considerations:

1) On balance, the answer to distaff equality in Canadian politics is "yes" and "no". What could be more balanced than that? Except there are now more women than men.

2) Women get into politics in order to make life better for other people. It is to laugh! That is not what politics is all about.

3) As a veteran pol can attest, it's more democratic to govern in secret. Remember that old saw about no woman being able to keep a secret? (Not many men, either, but that's beside the point.)

4) Government is hard work, and politicans work by the sweat of their brows. Women don't sweat—they glisten. But they also get a lot of things done: like running the house, the kids, and probably a job. And a man. This bears consideration.

5) Women, also according to mythology, get bogged down by details. But then they do have a lot of details to attend to (see above). As for men, of course, we never become unglued by such particulars as "Catch 22, sub-paragraph A-1-17". We just develop ulcers or have nervous breakdowns. Or strokes.

6) Women are frequently too clever by half. The ancient adage "Behind every good man stands a better woman" bespeaks a profound truth. Just suppose Maureen McTeer, for example, were elected to the Commons. Who would take the place of (as a Grit Cabinet Minister's wife was once dubbed) "The Power Behind the Drone"? But who needs Drones, anyway?

7) We could continue by paraphrasing the famous (and American!) curmudgeon, Fran Lebowitz, by saying, "designer jeans", "educational television", "adult entertainment", "parental guidance", "Canadian movies", "Pay-TV", and "female politicians" are all chilling examples of terminological inexactitude, or contradictions in terms.

As we said above, the issue is a thorny one, and we admit to being troubled by it. We are frankly reluctant to encourage females to strive for a Commons seat. We have too much respect for women to allow them to descend from their plinths to partake in the political mud-slinging and wrestling matches that ensue in this extinguished forum.

Why, the behaviour and quality of debate and thought is about as pure as the drinking water in Regina. No, no: we wish to have no truck with subjecting the fairer sex to the type of nasty invective that even — we are ashamed to recall — our own John Diefenbaker reverted to, when he once hissed that Flora was the finest woman ever to walk the streets of Kingston.

Gentlemen, we are the New Tories; sensitive to the tender feelings of the opposite sex.

We have faith that our position — visionary — missionary — Tory — will satisfy the girls. And that they will, in due course, return to stoically assume their rightful places: to lie back and think of England.

If it's good enough for Mila, then it should be good enough for the rest of them. Let's face it: the only important issues that should come from women are children.

The Scrum and How to Scrape It Off

Some of you may not be familiar with the scrum. It is a term referring to the newspaper reporters and TV and radio hacks who hang around the corridors of the House of Commons like ants around a picnic. (They are just as irritating, but are potentially a *lot* more dangerous.)

They get their name from the rugger game, where men gather about in scrimmage. After a few unfortunate run-ins with the scrum, you may well feel like dropping the ''r'' in the term.

But it's not at all a laughing matter. These people can ruin your career. Look what the cartoonist did to poor Bob Stanfield, when he pictured him with a banana! Look what the photographer did to poor Bob Stanfield, when he caught him fumbling a football! Look what the entire press corps did to poor Joe Clark, when all he did was not call Parliament back to session for six months, talk of selling Petrocan, promise to move the Canadian Embassy from Tel Aviv to Jerusalem, and talk of raising gas prices eighteen cents per gallon!

And that is precisely our point: The scrum will actually report what they see and hear, and we can't allow that to happen! Otherwise, they might well catch Stanfield eating a banana, fumbling a football, or Joe Clark, etc.

The following is a salient (important) list on the scrum. Read it and weep. Then read it and *be aware*. And remember that the difference between ''be aware'' and ''beware'' is merely a single letter. So, for that matter, is the difference between ''scrum'' and ''scum''.

1) WHAT DO SCRUM LOOK LIKE?

They tend to be beady-eyed, deceitful-looking, mean-spirited, and are usually clutching a pen and a pad of paper. (The really dangerous ones are clutching a crayon, because where they come from they're not trusted with sharp, pointed objects.)

So much for the newspaper and magazine reporters. The ones who are clutching microphones, with tape recorders around their necks, and/or being followed by portapack cameras, are the easiest to recognize beyond the mike: they are all good-looking—even the radio reporters. This has to do with the strange ethics of broadcasting, which we won't go into here except to say that it's not much different from politics. Dick Nixon had a funny nose and a five-o'clock shadow, and Joe had a weak chin, and we all know what the press did to *them*, don't we? So just thank the Good Lord that Brian has a chin like the Great Wall of China, and read on:

2) WHAT DO SCRUM DO?

They write unfair and inaccurate stories.

3) WHY DO THEY DO THIS?

They are just doing their job; trying to make a living; following the orders of their immediate superiors (a defence which was thrown out at the Nuremberg Trials, by the way); and, most important, a lot of them are out to bring in the NDP.

4) WHAT IS THE DUTY OF THE SCRUM?

To provide a window on Parliament.

5) WHAT IS OUR DUTY?

To dirty up that window as much as possible.

6) WHO DO YOU ACCUSE WHEN, AFTER THE SCRUM LEAVES, YOU DISCOVER YOUR WALLET IS MISSING?

No one. You shut up and hope that a reporter from the *Toronto Star* is caught at the Bay next week, purchasing a porn magazine with one of your credit cards.

7) WHY CAN'T I CRY OUT, OR CALL FOR THE POLICE, OR AT THE VERY LEAST UNLEASH THE RCMP?

Simple. Remember when Joe lost his luggage? No one attacked the airline for being stupid or sloppy, did they? Everyone declared a field day on poor Joe, as if it were *his* fault he entrusted his luggage so foolishly, and as if none of the reporters would do anything but hold onto *their* suitcases, cameras, and tripods during the entire flight.

There is a key lesson here: An MP can do no right. A reporter can do no wrong. Remember this, and you just may live long enough to die a natural death in the Senate.

How to Foil the Scrum
One of the greatest concerns of all politicians is the following: how to condense all his thoughts on a 12,000-page research document into an exciting, glib, uncontroversial thirty-second TV news spot. (Or: Chirpspeak.)

This is so important that it almost deserves a chapter of its own. But let's try to cover it here.

Sample question:

1) "MR. _____ ? COULD YOU PLEASE CONDENSE YOUR THOUGHTS ON THAT MASSIVE NEW REPORT ON _____ ? WE'VE JUST GOT THIRTY SECONDS!"

"This proposed bill is designed to give ordinary Canadians untold benefits. It's the finest piece of legislation that I know of. It not only features the application of my duly considered principles of dynamic probity, but also interfaces all aspects of this unusually complex question. We feel very positive about this bill, its resultant stimulus to the economy, and its easing of one of the most perplexing health problems to inflict personkind that this country, or any other in the Free World, has been forced to face."

(NB: the above has been used to answer, in thirty seconds, questions that range from abortion to capital punishment to wage-and-price controls and non-smoking sections in pubs. Memorize it.)

Another possible answer:

2) "WE'VE GOT JUST FIFTEEN SECONDS BEFORE WE LOSE OUR SATELLITE. COULD YOU TELL US JUST EXACTLY WHAT YOU MEAN?"

"Certainly! Our government stands firm in its resolve to better the lot of ordinary Canadians with progressive legislation such as this implies. Our government, with true altruistic humanism, is pledged to give every man, woman, and child in this great land the rewards that are their rightful due." (If you wish to be witty, add "Postage due, however, is another matter!")

3) A preliminary note on this one, which could be described as "the intellectual approach": it is dangerous, but it has been used successfully by a certain blue-eyed Bay Street lawyer who left a sinking government ship back in the mid-1970s, and attempted a comeback less than a decade later:

"MR. TURNER," (ooops — gave it away) "COULD YOU GIVE US A FEW COMMENTS ABOUT THIS QUESTION? WE'VE ONLY GOT A FEW SECONDS!"

"Gentlemen, I'm not about to encapsulate my views just in order to slide into your evening snapshot of news. This issue is far too complex, too many-sided, too profound to give you a flat "yes" or "no". I'm afraid, gentlemen, that you can't fool me into short-changing such a major, substantive issue in just a few short seconds! Good day/night/ grief!"

A beauty, huh? We hate to steal it from the Grits, but God knows how often they've stolen *our* great ideas! Remember how they mocked Bob for his wage-and-price-controls concept in 1974, and then rushed them into action just a few months later? Well, two can play at that game, boys!

How to Handle the Men and Women of the Press

As we used to say back in college, how do you make love to a porcupine? (Answer: very carefully.) We are here about to save your future, so read carefully and memorize everything.

YOU ARE BEING QUESTIONED BY BARBARA FRUM:

Very important! Remember *The Journal*! Remember most people don't read any more! But also remember Frum only has about three minutes to do you in, since there will more than likely be a Grit and a socialist up there as well.

Right now, however, Barbara has backed you into a corner. Begin by saying, "Let me answer that question, Mary Lou, by telling you that. . . ." (She'll be speechless, for a nice change.) Or try this one: "Gee, Keith, when I hear a question like that, I don't think you're being fair to our native people. . . ." (This is a real winner. First, she'll be outraged you confused her with Morrison. Secondly, she would sooner die than be accused of being unfair to our native people.) Another good ploy: "Aw, come on Barbara, do you think Mary Lou would ask a below-the-belt question like that?" (Sisterhood is too powerful for that one. Would Frum admit that M.L. is less capable of punches than she?) Or try belittling: "C'mon Barb! I thought you were tough! You're just pawing the air!" (By the time she reaches for a longer knife, a commercial may have come along.) Or ask about her loved ones: "How's Murray? Anything new in the African art collection? *Love* David's pieces in *Saturday Night*!" Try the legal angle: "Barbara, you know that's *sub judice*! It's before the courts!" (As a typical CBCer Frum wouldn't dream of breaking the law!)

When really down and out, grab at straws: "I'm really surprised, Barbara, that a person like yourself, a member of an oppressed group — women — would want to oppress a nice guy like me." (As a libber, Frum may well be thrown by the thought she is harming the relations between the sexes.) And, if all else fails, feign laryngitis. Respond to her dirty questions by writing your answers on cue cards. Remember two things: She faces a blank screen, electronically filled in on home TVs by the miracles of modern science (or at least until we Tories get our knives into the CBC budget). So she can't see you — and she can't read your replies!

YOU ARE BEING QUESTIONED BY JACK WEBSTER OF VANCOUVER:

Relax. You won't understand a word he's saying. Just mumble "I waive consecutive translation" and sit there smiling. His brogue is so thick the Russians have considered using it to replace the Berlin Wall, and the Americans have considered using it to send uncoded yet indecipherable messages to troops overseas.

YOU ARE BEING QUESTIONED BY ALLAN FOTHERINGHAM:

Flatter the SOB to death. Tell him you always read *Maclean's* from back to front, because of his witty, acerbic columns. Better yet, tell him the only reason you take *Maclean's* is in order to read his witty, acerbic columns. Anyway, don't worry about him; he's been defanged. He hated the Grits even more than we do, and Brian's got him in his pocket. Just smile, flatter him, act as if you think he's a lot taller than he really is, and flatter him some more. He's got the world's tallest free-standing ego.

YOU ARE BEING QUESTIONED BY BARBARA AMIEL:

Try not to stare at her chest too much, although this will be hard. Tell her how proud you are that she is the editor of a major newspaper, even though she is a woman. Mention that you thought her autobiography wasn't half as embarrassing to read as Margaret Trudeau's. Tell her you are proud to live in a country where her views can be tolerated, and that you will defend to your death her right to express them. And mention, *but only in passing*, that you are particularly delighted that Canada's William Buckley is so much better looking than America's. Offer her some codeine; she's a sucker for it.

YOU ARE BEING QUESTIONED BY CHARLES LYNCH:

Tell him you loved his best-selling book, *You Can't Print That!*, and would have paid for it had you not received a copy from a friend. Tell him you think he is far funnier and more acerbic than Allan Fotheringham, and it's a bloody shame that Foth gets so much press and he doesn't. *Do not tell him that you love his witty, acerbic columns in Maclean's.*

YOU ARE BEING QUESTIONED BY MIKE DUFFY:

Tell him he's lost some weight and looks good. Tell him he's gotten taller and looks good. Tell him that, with his weight loss, he looks so much taller. Don't tell him anything else, especially about politics. Like most political reporters, he'll eat you alive; unlike most other political reporters, he *won't* spit you out. Duffy's been around for years and he's getting rounder every day.

YOU ARE BEING QUESTIONED BY KNOWLTON NASH:

Tell him you love his new glasses. Ask him if he is a natural blonde. Ask him how Lorraine is. Ask him if he has really been married seven times, or was that a misprint. Tell him you think *The National* is vastly improved. Tell him again how much you love his new glasses.

YOU ARE BEING QUESTIONED BY DAVID HALTON:

Tell him you thought his father was the finest journalist this country ever had. Tell him he has the strangest Saskatchewan accent you've ever heard. Tell him you'll speak to Barbara Frum and no one else.

YOU ARE BEING QUESTIONED BY NORM PERRY:

Tell him you think he's the best interviewer in Canadian TV. Tell him you think he is a living example of how you can rise to the top of TV journalism without being cute, and this is a blow against the silly concern with surface on television. Tell him you love his new glasses. Tell him *Perry's Probe* was the best show on TV, and ask when it will be coming back.

YOU ARE BEING QUESTIONED BY PAM WALLINS:

Try not to be overwhelmed by her cheekbones — they are potentially as dangerous as Barbara Amiel's breasts. Don't let her beauty faze you; she's a dangerous interviewer, and that is all you should be concerned about, you sexist pig, you. Tell her you've always been fascinated with the fact that the finest reporters come from Saskatchewan (herself; Foth; Richard Brown; Keith Morrison). Tell her you can't cope with so much beauty that early in the morning. Tell her you will only speak with Norm

Perry, because he's been interviewing you since before she was born.

YOU ARE BEING QUESTIONED BY MARY LOU FINLAY:

Tell her how relieved you are that she is interviewing you, rather than Barbara Frum. Tell her how much you like her new hairdo. Tell her you don't blame her for leaving her home town of Ottawa, and you personally wish you could escape it more often. Tell her you want to be the father of her children. Tell her that under the new Charter of Rights you don't have to answer without a lawyer present. Tell her you preferred her on *Live It Up*. Tell her she sounds like Elizabeth Grey.

YOU ARE BEING QUESTIONED BY ELIZABETH GREY:

Tell her how much she sounds like Mary Lou Finlay. Call her Barbara. Tell her you vastly prefer radio. Tell her how much you used to love her on Don Harron's *Morningside* when she did weekly reports from Ottawa. Tell her you think her husband is one of the finest journalists in the country. Tell her you think her husband is the only journalist in the country. Tell her you think she is vastly superior to Barbara Frum. Tell her you love her new hairdo. (If she is interviewing you over the phone, this last one may strike her as insincere.)

YOU ARE BEING QUESTIONED BY KEITH MORRISON:

Tell him that, even though you are determinedly heterosexual, you find him to be the handsomest man you've ever met in your life. This will throw him off so much, he'll only ask you soft, puffy questions, and you will be safe until Frum gets back home from vacation.

YOU ARE BEING QUESTIONED BY YOUR WIFE:

Tell her that the meeting ran late; that autograph hounds kept you going long past when you thought you'd get out; that she is the only one for you; that if she divorces you she'll get nothing, since your career will be in tatters, and the children will starve. Tell her you love her new hairdo. Tell her all the best wives come from Saskatchewan. (Use this last one only on wives who come from Saskatchewan.)

Some Last Clues to Success in Handling Journalists Before They Manhandle You:

1) Never be direct when you can be indirect. The longest distance between two points is obfuscation. (See Chapter Three.)

2) Remember, in the journalism business, no news is good advertising. If you are too controversial you may alienate some of the people who pay for the rag or the program. So keeping your mouth shut is in *their* favour as much as it is in yours. Be partners in crime; make one another happy; shut up.

3) There are no investigative journalists in Canada. Bernstein and Woodward are south of the border; we are north. The only things Canadian journalists dig are Culture Club and Canadian Club, and not necessarily in that order.

4) Remember: there is no such thing as "off the record". Sneeze, and the bastards will print "*Gezundheit*" on page 1. *Think* before you cosy up to a reporter. Remember that loving porcupine, noted above. If the reporter were William Tell, would you let him take an apple from your head with a blunderbuss? We rest our case.

The National Museums of Canada

No, no, we're *not* talking about the Senate, here. You see, the previous government combined all the national museums under a single banner. And we think the colour of the banner was white, as in surrender. (Remember what a knockout job Paul Hellyer did with the Armed Forces?)

The National Gallery of Canada, for instance, is the only one that has its own Head of Publications, a Production Manager, and six editors (three in each of our two beloved languages, natch). They are still trying to figure out if it should just continue to churn out art catalogues, or become a kind of monster Museums' Publications Department. Maybe putting out the artistic equivalent of the *Toronto Sun*, with pictures of

Culture Quiz: Who Are These Men?

1) Is this:
   A. A Welfare bum
   B. A CBC producer
   C. Gordon Pinsent
   D. An artist

2) Is this:
   A. A Bay Street
      ambassador
   B. An artist
   C. A civil servant

3) Is this:
    A. Deputy Minister of
       Sports and Recreation
    B. Deputy Minister of
       Finance
    C. An artist

4) Is this:
    A. A con artist
    B. Provincial Deputy
       Minister of Finance
    C. Provincial Treasury
       Bills

Answer 1. A, B, C and D
        2. C
        3. C
        4. A and B

scantily clad sculptures as Sunshine Art?

Then there is the problem of what to build, when to build it, and where. There is, at the time of this writing, a very large hole on Parliament Hill, which means that either there was a war and we missed it, or they are about to start building something. And guess who is going to be paying for this?

Finally, the NGC has about 95 % of its collection underground, which is just super for surviving nuclear war, but rather lousy if people wish to view the stuff. We think it might be helpful if every Member of Parliament — that's nearly 300 right there — were obligated to carry or lug or drag a different piece to Question Period each day, and hold it up to the cameras for the television-viewing public to see. It'd be a great chance to bring culture to *hoi polloi*, and air the stuff out. Plus, we'd be able to point to this as an example of artistic TV, and one more reason why the CBC is no longer needed. (See The CBC — but not too often.)

The CBC

Can it. If the socialists want their own radio and TV network, let them pay for it themselves and not demand hundreds of millions from public funds.

Aside from *Tommy Hunter* and *Front Page Challenge*, what else is there? The only interesting show we've ever caught live on the Corp. was CBC reporters dancing for joy during the Parti Québecois victory in 1976 — and they weren't supposed to be on camera.

I say let ABC, CBS, and NBC handle our entertainment needs. They always have, anyway. And as far as *Hockey Night in Canada* is concerned, we've kind of lost interest, what with the decline of the Montreal Canadiens' dynasty and all.

Get rid of it. With the money saved, maybe we'll finally be able to afford some really nifty new battleships or nuclear weapons. (See Chapter Six.) Now *that* is communication.

CHAPTER NINE

How *We* Can Make It Work!

Changes in the Civil Service, Or, Squeezing the Mandarins

It is hell to come out and take a stand for something. Still, we, the leaders and policy-makers of the National Progressive Conservative Party of this magnificent land, believe that tinkering with the civil service (or squeezing the Mandarins, which is like getting blood from a turnip) is an essential part and duty of our mandate. (Okay, okay, persondate. Thanks for that, Maureen.)

In 1982, there were about 583,752 public servants working for the Federal Government. Sorry, make that 583,752 public servants. (Whether they were working or not is part of the problem, is it not?)

But that's a lot, you'll have to admit. It's at least a dozen more than are employed at Buckingham Palace, and Great Britain has many more millions of population than we do. And, we may add, our Canadian civil servants do *not* change the Old Guard on any regular basis. Or wear snappy outfits.

The budget for all this was $83 billion. As Réal Caouette, may his soul twist in peace, was fond of saying, "Dat's a lot ov money. See all doze zeros?"

Approximately 15% of that went to salaries. The other 85% went to more empire-building and maintenance than has been carried out by, collectively, the British, the Americans, the Soviets, and the ancient Greeks and Romans.

There are, of course, the watchdogs: the Treasury Board, the Public Service Commission, etc; watchdogs bred for their sensitive snouts; trained to sniff out fiscal skulduggery with their relentless tracking ability; ingrained with so fierce a viciousness that a found-out fiscal cut-purse (or bureaucratic buccaneer) would be in grave danger of being gummed to death.

The toughest dog of the bunch is a real son-of-a-bitch: the Auditor-General. The buck privateers stop here. Although, to be fair, this dog is more of a pointer than anything else. Injuries are usually sustained from getting his tale in one's eye.

By most accounts, the civil service is quite well run. Like most huge corporations, however, it is top-heavy with senior executives. In fact, there are so many Chiefs, the Department of Indian Affairs was bidding to take over.

It has been thought that "the key to good government is to remove as much power as possible from the lower levels of the bureaucracy." (The body of the South American dictator who said this was recently dug up; clearly his underlings were displeased.) So, as you can see, this may work well in theory — but theories (see Chapter Five) have a nasty habit of being just that. (Theories. Are you paying attention?)

Good managers are the clever persons who short-circuit the impasse systems and get things done. That's why we have trains that manage to run, not to mention almost on time. Sometimes. (To be brutally frank, we were going to say See Chapter on Via Rail, but it was sent to our Ottawa Strategy Office by train from the west coast and has yet to arrive.)

Enough of Philosophy 101. What does the civil service comprise? And how is it structured? So glad you asked!

MINISTER: Usually a lawyer; usually knows absolutely nothing about the department he/she is in charge of. (He would know positively nothing about the department, except that he is not quite positive about anything.) He is never in the department long enough to learn its purpose and function(s), and if, by some fluke, he *has* learned something, he is quickly moved out.

Is in charge of general policy guidelines. Specific policy guidelines would entail far too much knowledge of the department; see paragraph above.

DEPUTY MINISTER: A career civil servant who knows and runs the department. He never lets principles, morality, or the Minister get in the way of good government. He is confident in the realization that he is more immovable than the Pope, and, since the first Vatican Council, just as infallible.

ASSISTANT DEPUTY MINISTER: Another career civil servant, beholden and responsible to the Deputy Minister and fervently wishing for the latter's demise. He/she is captain of the various parts of the department, serving somewhat like a quasi- (and occasionally queasy) vice-president of a large company. A large company whose assets are nil, whose liabilities are bottomless, and whose records are secret. It's like dying and going to heaven, when you think of it.

DIRECTOR-GENERAL: Third in command, usually in charge of a number of sections of the department that have a common element to bunch them together. Fervently awaiting the early deaths of the Deputy Minister and Assistant Deputy Minister.

CHIEF or MANAGER: Rules one part of a division and kowtows to the director (which is excellent background for working in the Ministry of Agriculture, for example).

SPECIAL ASSISTANT TO THE DEPUTY MINISTER: The only impressive aspect of this bureaucrat's existence is the high salary. And his main function is to collect his paycheque. Like housework — someone has to do it.

SPECIAL ADVISER/EXECUTIVE CONSULTANT: Two alternate spellings of "Special Assistant to the Deputy Minister."

CLERKS (1-4), TYPISTS (1-4), SECRETARIES (1-4), GOFERS (1): The people who have to do all the work and follow restraint guidelines.

"Well," said Jason Robards, after the nuclear holocaust in *The Day After*, "we've got our work cut out for us!" I mean, how do we tinker with all this? When you really think of it, Jason Robards had it easy; he could start again; start *over*.

But how do *we* squeeze the Mandarins, and not throw out the cry-babies with the bathwater, to coin a phrase?

With some deliberation, here are our suggested changes that will be *seen* to be believed:

1) The most obvious change: those without beards will grow them. Distaff bureaucrats are exempted, unless competitiveness with male counterparts forces them to employ a novelty item, such as a false beard. Testosterone injections will be appreciated, but hardly necessary.

   Those already with beards will shave.

   Some will have to get into leather.

   Some out of it.

   Some into dresses.

   Some out of them.

   Some into tweeds.

   Some out of sync.

   We realize that these changes are drastic, and in some cases startling. But we have to start somewhere.

2) We will restrain overspending on the civil service by rewarding initiative, ingenuity, and productivity with a variation of the Baden-Powell Sash.

   You read right; public servants in the Tory administration will be able to accumulate scores of merit badges. After quilting the sash with considerable meritorious patchwork, the individual overachiever will be given an all-expense paid vacation to the local National Park of his or her choice. (Parks Canada thought that one up.)

We hope that this scheme results in the exorcism of the Sisyphus complex so endemic to the civil service. (For those of you to whom that reference was Greek, Sisyphus was a king of Corinth doomed in Hades to roll a stone uphill which always rolled down again. Ring a bell?)

3) Grit hacks will be fired immediately.

4) Socialists hacks will be fired the day before the Grit hacks.

Yes, we know we will receive criticism for our efforts. But believe us when we state, categorically, that we will temper our changes with fairness and high resolve, and we will *not* be seen to rub the noses of high muckety-mucks in the dirt of political expediency, the polls willing.

The Reshaping of Ottawa

It has been a long and lonely time in political exile, fellows, and we are most anxious, and understandably so, to establish our imprint on the nation's capital. But our changes, so long in coming, will be more than merely a matter of style:

1) The Peace Tower will be lowered by the spring of 1985, so as to stretch awesomely before the House of Commons, like a suppliant before its master.

Why, you ask? Because Tory strategists — who have had lots of time to think about this, let us remind you — feel that the erect tower presents a goading reminder to ordinary Canadians of the former Prime Minister (the Rt. Honourable P.E. Trudeau; so soon they forget), and his famous middle finger.

No longer. Extended horizontally before Parliament, the

Peace Tower will now be symbolic of Brian's chin, a thrilling new beckoning structure leading up to the opening (read: mouth) whence all blessings flow. In other words, the Grit curse is about to be replaced by the Tory blessing.

2) We will continue with the construction of such buildings as the new National Gallery, *Le Musée National de l'Aviation*, and the National Museum of Man. (The women will just have to wait their turn.)

To these new homes for Canadian treasures, we hope to add a *Salon des Incompétents*. This imposing structure, which will *not* be built by Arthur Erickson, will eventually house a stunning collection of dinosaurs, including visual histories of Crown Corporations, Public Works schemes, films of Mirabel Airport on a busy day when dozens of people make their way through the cavernous, echoing halls, and other Liberal memorabilia.

Who says that we Tories wish to destroy that which went before us? *Au contraire, mon frère!* We hope to build a continual reminder of what they did to this country!

3) We *will* permit, in a classic show of Progressive Conservative magnanimity, the *exclusive* use of the Rideau Canal for ice-skating by the official Opposition — from 6 a.m. to 8 p.m., for the months of July and August. (Johnny-on-the-spot change-huts only on request.)

Confidential Canada (Con-Can)

We plan to create this department just as soon as we complete our takeover of Ottawa. Next to Revenue Canada, it will be the repository of the greatest amount of information about and by Canadians in the Federal Government. We hope you will come to regard Con-Can as a sort of comforting Neighbourhood Watch — your kindly neighbours in Ottawa keeping an eye out for you.

There is, of course, the current *Access to Information Act* which the

Grits brought in early in this decade. They were forced to do it because of all the grumbling from a lot of disgruntled misanthropes. We even grumbled a bit ourselves. But, fellow Tories, we have to admit that things look a lot different from the other end of the binoculars. (With budget cuts, it will be telescopes, of course.)

However, let us assure you that once we get the bugs out of the system, there will be a lot fewer secrets!

Trust us!

With the Grits, it all got to be too Hollywood for words. If the Canadian people want to know about anything, there should be all kinds of legitimate ways for them to find out: Stats Can, for instance. *ABC World Report*, with Peter Jennings, who was born in Canada, after all. The local public library.

Confidential Canada should be the answer. We've had quite enough of the official secrecy actions of the Grits over the past few decades, or however long they have been in power. No, we Tories are going to do things differently: Any Canadian, of any political hue, should be able to obtain any information he or she desires about the actions of the federal government and its employees, providing that it in no way impinges upon the need for secrecy on the part of that Government and/or its employees.

As a great Protestant leader may or may not have said, in a different language, nearly half a millenium ago; *Here We Stand!*

Snoop and Peek Department (Spy Canada)

OPERATION TOP WATCH

RESEARCH AND DESTROY MISSIONS

BACK-DOOR DEPARTMENT

SECURITY-CAN

Call it what you will, we are severely troubled by this. Whatever happened to our Redcoats in their endless quest for Turncoats?

Even in these post-McCarthy days, when our Redcoats are sporting brown coats, we Tories find ourselves deeply tugged by the RCMP motto, *"Maintiens le droit,"* or *"Gardes le droit,"* or, for those handful of you who are not yet fluently bilingual, "Preserve the Conservatives!"

So the question is: Why do we need to let our civil service George Smileys be our umbrellas?

We're somewhat ambivalent about this one. It smacks too much of Kaplanism. As the old saw goes, why should we adopt a third-rate idea from the Liberals when we can probably get a second-rate one from the NDP?

We suppose our own Canadian Security and Intelligence Service will have to stay, but it's somewhat unsettling to contemplate an FBI man under every bed, and our own, all-Canadian Central Intelligence Agency, or CI, eh?

The Senate: Reform or Reward?

What do you think? Is the Pope Polish? Is Canada cold? Is Ottawa dull? Are the Grits arrogant?

Let's put it this way, for those of you who have the misfortune of being educated in this country, we plan to reform the Senate just as quickly as the Grits did over the past century. Of course, it will be hard to find someone who was jailed for destroying a $2-million-dollar computer, but we'll try; we'll try. We simply won't make that a prerequisite for sitting in the Senate, that's all.

Further Comments on the Tory Policy on the Arts

Art, as every Tory knows, is a nasty business. The image of grown men hopping about in leotards, women throwing cans of paint at giant canvases, fat people screaming at the top of their lungs in strange languages — it's all kind of silly, we think.

Not only that, but all the so-called artists (we'll leave out the quotation marks, in kindness) appear to be rolling in dough — think of Toni Onley — while all they do is cry for more money. To paraphrase a former politician, "Why Should We Sell Their Canvases/Shows/Tickets?"

Let's face it; we are under no obligation to help them out if they just happen to be overdrawn at the Art Bank.

Now, there can be exceptions. For instance, if an artist paints wheat fields filled with socialists pulling broken combines, we might be willing to shell out a few bucks to put it on a wall. Which wall, we won't say.

Beyond taste, beyond critical standards, beyond everything, there is an ethical question involved with government support for the arts, and it should be spelled out here: Most of them don't vote Conservative. This should never be forgotten, when they ask for our hands to move to the purse strings.

One final thought: It is questionable whether there are any artists in this country *at all*. The true artists, as we have all been taught from youth, end up in Los Angeles.

Who's the Mandarin?

A.

C.

D.

If You Guessed:

A. An impenetrable brick wall, you're wrong.

B. A bone-head, you're wrong.

C. A technocrat, you're wrong.

D. A genius, you're wrong.

E. A saint, you're wrong.

It's F. Mandarin shoes nailed to the office floor. See Mandarins re: immovable.

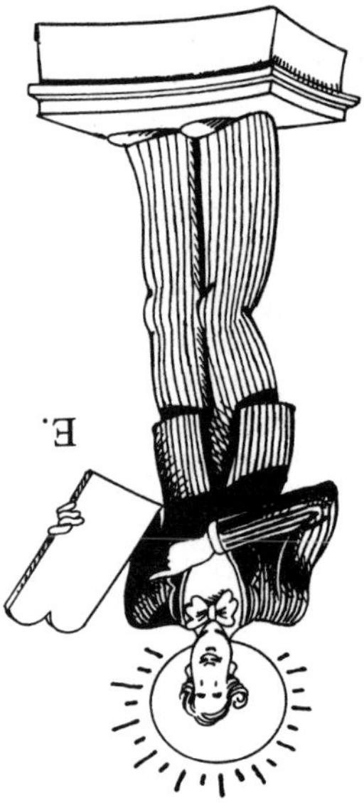

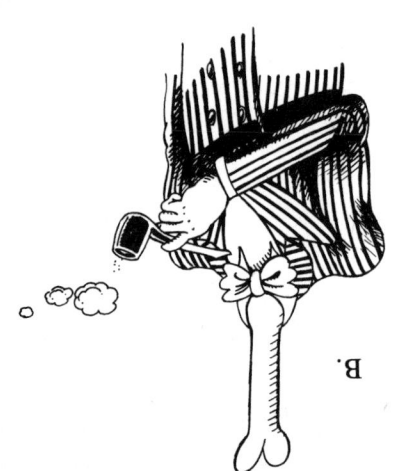

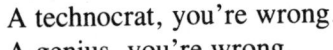

What We Have Learned from Past Tory Successes, from John A. Macdonald to Joe Clark, Which We Plan to Use and Carry On in the Future:

CHAPTER TEN

What Shall We Do With Joe?

Joe Must Go Somewhere!

Don't laugh. One of the most admirable things about the Chinese and the Jews is that they take very good care of their elderly, indigent, sick. We could learn a lot from them.

Which brings us to the painful subject at hand: What shall we do with the Right Honourable Joseph P. Clark, who, after all, ran this country, without incurring many debts, political or financial, back in the late 1970s and early 1980s? (You can see just how easy it is to be generous.)

We are not talking about a senior citizen here; we are not talking about a retiring head of a party. We are talking about a young man, still in his forties, still in control of all his faculties, or at least as much in control of his faculties as he was just a few short years ago.

Which may be part of the problem at hand. He's still a bit youthful to play the role of elder statesman. And, unlike Richard Nixon, he may well want to try for the top spot again, God forbid.

So what do we do with him? Pierre Trudeau, if you'll pardon the vulgarity, took his arch-enemy, John Turner, and plunked him down in the high-profile and extremely difficult position of Finance Minister. And look what happened! Less than a decade later, Turner ran for the top job and found he had no option. Do we want this to happen to us?

Which brings us back to the problem at hand, and a handy problem it is, too: What should we do with Joe?

More cynical Tories might recommend what Peter Demeter did to his wife, or what someone must have done to Jimmy Hoffa. But we Tories don't act like that. It would be unconscionably immoral. And anyway, American hit-men usually ask for their money up front — and in U.S. dollars — which can run up a pretty steep bill.

Okay, it comes down to this: Joe Clark is ready, willing, and more than available to take on any job which is commensurate with his background, skills, and intelligence.

I know what you are thinking. So try some of these:

— Send Joe Clark to be the Assistant High Commissioner to Australia, where he would be in charge of apologizing for the actions and words of Ed and Lily Schreyer.

Arguments for: Australia is on the other side of the globe.

Arguments against: Australia is still on the planet Earth.

— Send Joe Clark to solve the sectarian violence in Lebanon.

Arguments for: he could get hurt.

Arguments against: he might not get hurt.

— Send Joe Clark to work out a peace agreement between Iraq and a hard place.

Arguments for: it's half-way around the world, and the job could take many years to achieve.

Arguments against: Khomeini could die, Iran could sue for peace, and Joe could win the Nobel Prize for Peace and get on the cover of *Maclean's*.

— Send Joe Clark to medical school, have him earn a psychoanalytical degree, and send him to Libya to treat Muammar al-Gaddafi for insanity.

Arguments for: medical school can take up to a decade; psychoanalysis, of the classical Freudian kind, can take many, many years.

Arguments against: absolutely none.

As you can see, we have a problem here, and it is in many ways as difficult to solve as getting the budget deficit down to a few bucks.

We have to count on *you*. If you have any real brainstorms, call 996-WHOM in Ottawa (area code 613), and tell us what *you* think we should do with Joe.

And—one more favour, before you read any further. We've typed up a simple form on the next page. Please fill it in, tear it out, and mail to:

> JOE JOBS
> P.O. Box 1980
> Postal Station Eh?
> Ottawa, Ontario
> K0P OUT

Form on Joe Clark's Future:

I, MP FOR _____,

BELIEVE JOE CLARK SHOULD GO TO _____

WITH THE INTENTION OF _____

AND PROBABLY _____ AGAIN

FOR AT LEAST _____ YEARS/DECADES.

Respectfully submitted,

_____
(Signature here)

CHAPTER ELEVEN

Be Prepared! But Let's Add a Cautionary Note!

A Prime Minister Quiz

After all the complex theorizing we've been going through, and the heavy memorizing of speeches, one-liners, and obfuscations, you probably feel you need a well-deserved break.

Well, here it is. Enjoy this quiz. And you will find how to rate your answers at the end of the quiz.

Q. How many prime ministers of Canada have been lawyers?

A. Twelve of the eighteen prime ministers, including Brian and John Turner. Yet even though two-thirds of our PMs *have* been attorneys, it is interesting to note that not one of them has been jailed or driven from office.

Q. What was Sir John A. Macdonald's favourite nickname for himself?

A. "Old Tomorrow".

Q. What is Joe Clark's least favourite nickname for himself?

A. "Young Yesterday".

Q. What Conservative Prime Minister held office for less than ten weeks?

A. Sir Charles Tupper. If you said Joe Clark, take off 5 points.

Q. Where did Sir John A. Macdonald live before he became Prime Minister?

A. In Kingston, Ontario. If you said "Bellevue House", give yourself an extra 10 points. If you said "Over at Flora's", subtract 20 points.

Q. Who was the sixteenth Prime Minister of this great country?

A. Joe Clark. Give yourself 10 points if you *missed* that one!

Q. How does Ronald Reagan, through his economic policies, constantly remind Americans of John Diefenbaker? (This is a toughie; be warned.)

A. Reagan practises Voodoo Economics, and Dief allowed Voodoo planes on Canadian soil, though only with non-nuclear Falcon missiles. Give yourself 25 points, if you got this one.

Q. How was Sir Mackenzie Bowell a remarkable Prime Minister (1894-96)?

A. He was viciously anti-Catholic, paranoid, a blowhard and dumb. Today, you couldn't rise above the level of back-bencher with a background like that.

Q. How is the name "Schefferville" relevant to a Prime Minister?

A. Who put this one in here? Is there a mole in our office? What's going on?

Q. How many seats did John Diefenbaker win in the wonderful election of 1958?

A. He won 208 out of 265. Until Brian, it was the largest majority ever.

Q. How did R. B. Bennett, the Prime Minister of this great country from 1930 to 1935, die?

A. He was found dead in his bathtub, which made him cleaner in death than most Grit Prime Ministers in life.

Q. How much money did John A. Macdonald and his cronies receive from a rich shipowner in 1872, to help him in his 1872 campaign?

A. Only a lousy $350,000! And all John A. did for the guy, Sir Hugh Allan, was to award him the contract to build the Canadian Pacific Railway! Just look at how much more we can take in nowadays, without having to promise a fraction as much! Be thankful you live in the 1980s; poor John A. had a scandal on his hands for a lot less!

Q. How many seats did John Diefenbaker win in the magnificent election of 1958?

A. He grabbed 208 out of 265. We realize that this is the same answer as given above. But we wanted to see if you were concentrating, and also, to be frank, we like talking about it.

Q. What Tory Prime Minister called William Lyon Mackenzie King "the most contemptible charlatan ever to darken the annals of Canadian politics"?

A. Arthur Meighen, who ruled for only a few months in 1920, 1921, and 1926, but for that quote alone will live for ever.

Q. What shocking thing did Sir Joseph Caldwell Abbott (1891-1892) do when he was a young man?

A. He signed the Annexation Manifesto of 1849, which urged that Canada join the United States. It's good to know this, so that if things get rough economically over the next few years, Brian can always claim a precedent.

Q. What did John Crosbie describe his 1979 budget as?

A. "Short-term pain for long-term gain." Not too bright, John, but we thought we'd toss this one in just to tweak your nose a little.

Q. What was Sir Mackenzie Bowell, Prime Minister back in the 1890s, doing when he was ninety-four?

A. He was still an active member of the Canadian Senate. We're not surprised that he was still alive in his mid-nineties, but the idea that he was still *active* in the Senate really tickled us.

Q. What did Dief do on May 2, 1962?

A. He devalued the Canadian dollar to 92.5 cents U.S., and pegged it at that price. It shows the double standards of our left-wing press. Trudeau let it drift down more than 28 cents, and the reporters just mumbled, and speculated on foreign money markets.

Q. Who was the Mackenzie Tower in the West Block of the Parliament Buildings named after?

A. Alexander Mackenzie, a Liberal hack who was Prime Minister briefly in the 1870s, before John A. came roaring back to save our country. It just goes to show what empire builders those Grits are, building towers for their pimples on the face of Canadian history.

Q. Who is the greatest Prime Minister in Canadian history?

A. You didn't even have to ask. Brian thanks you, and expects to see you at the regular caucus meeting, next Tuesday.

Give yourself 5 points for each correct answer, except for those noted.

If you got 80-100, you are Prime Ministerial material (but only after Brian steps down. Shame on you).

If you got 60-80, you are Cabinet material.

If you got 40-60, you are back-bencher at best.

If you got 20-40, you probably supported Joe at the leadership convention back in June 1983.

If you got less than 20, well, there's always the Senate.

Just in Case . . . How to Convert this Page into a New Leadership Convention
Part 1

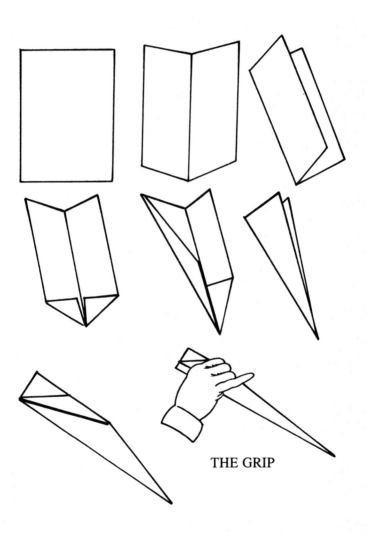

THE GRIP

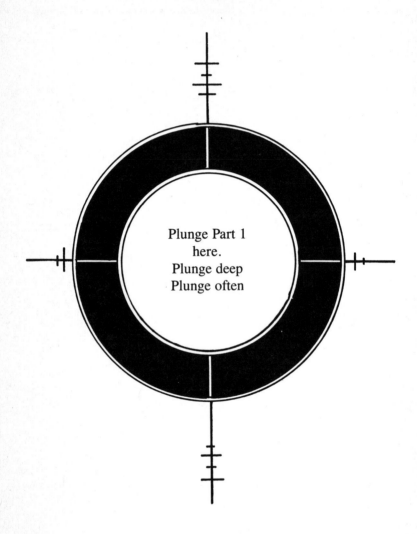

Plunge Part 1
here.
Plunge deep
Plunge often

N.B. You must supply your own tape.